Environmental Quality and Social Justice in Urban America

An exploration of conflict and concord among those who seek environmental quality and those who seek social justice

Edited by James Noel Smith

Environmental Quality and Social Justice in Urban America

Environmental Quality and Social Justice in Urban America

*An exploration of conflict and concord
among those who seek
environmental quality and those
who seek social justice*

Edited by James Noel Smith

THE CONSERVATION FOUNDATION | WASHINGTON, D.C.

THE CONSERVATION FOUNDATION *is a nonprofit organization broadly dedicated to encouraging human conduct to sustain and enrich life on earth. Since its founding in 1948, it has attempted to provide intellectual leadership in the cause of wise management of the earth's resources. Is is now focusing increasing attention on one of the critical issues of the day—how to use wisely that most basic resource, the land itself.*

The cover illustration is a rendering by Frank P. Higgins
of a photograph by John Kramer of Iowa City, Iowa,
whose permission for such use is gratefully acknowledged.

Additional copies of this book may be ordered by writing to:
PUBLICATIONS DEPARTMENT
THE CONSERVATION FOUNDATION
1717 MASSACHUSETTS AVENUE, N.W.
WASHINGTON, D. C. 20036

Contents

Foreword

THIS VOLUME is both an experiment and the result of an experiment. Just as the conference from which it is drawn was an exploration by men and women of good will into issues and questions rarely discussed in such a forum, so this book is largely a reflection of the views expressed there.

Some of the participants in the conference brought strong views with them, and gave passionate expression to them during the course of the meeting. Others, less certain, challenged and probed, hoping to illuminate for themselves and for others the nooks and crannies of the complex questions discussed.

The Conservation Foundation's purpose in convening this conference was to begin an intensive dialogue on how and where the views of persons seeking environmental quality as a primary goal coincide and conflict with the views of persons seeking social justice as a primary goal. "Both sides" were amply represented at the conference, and we believe that everyone present came away enriched by its content and its spirit. Moreover, we think that all of the participants left for home with their views adjusted— or reinforced.

One reason for the good talk was the relaxing atmosphere at the Woodstock Conference Center in Woodstock, Illinois, whose staff we would like to thank now for having made our stay there so pleasant and rewarding. The stay itself would not have been possible without the American Conservation Association's generous help in defraying the costs.

Our thanks go to James Noel Smith, a Senior Associate at the Conservation Foundation at the time of the conference and now Deputy Director of the National Commission on Water Quality. It was he who organized the conference and then combined the strands of conversation with supplementary essays to form this book.

We are also grateful to Timothy J. Adams, the Foundation's Director of Public Affairs, for putting the manuscript into final shape and for overseeing its production.

ARTHUR A. DAVIS
Vice President for Operations
The Conservation Foundation

Preface

THE FOCUS OF THIS BOOK is on the environmental movement and its position relative to other concerns in American society. Most specifically, it gives attention to a recent set of allegations. These are: that the goals and strategies of the environmental movement are somehow antithetical to those interests of society which are seeking social justice and equality of opportunity, and that an elite, upper-middle-class, exclusively white sector of America is using the environmental issue, either overtly or unconsciously, to protect its own "room at the top" from the encroachments of those less favorably placed on the social and economic ladder of American society.

At their most exaggerated, such contentions suggest the seeds of a kind of "class struggle"—the "haves" of American society versus the "have nots," with environmental quality protection as the social *raison d'être* by which the privileged and relatively wealthy solidify their elite position and implore the rest of society to accept economic scarcity and social immobility in the service of ecological principles. Far-fetched as this may seem, one cannot be oblivious to the increasing conflict that characterizes such topics as environmental-quality protection and jobs, low- and moderate-income housing, open-space and landscape protection, aesthetic taste versus utilitarian services, and, last but not least, that conundrum of how to make an equitable social distribution of the costs of pollution control.

The periodic eruption of such conflict—and the prospect of more to come, as stringent pollution-control requirements precipitate short-term economic displacements—is bringing the motives and the strategies of the environmental movement in for some sharp criticism. One senses that the public's enchantment with all things environmental is being succeeded by a cooler, more critical view. Some business and industrial interests have been quick to sense the strategic advantage in attacking environmentalists and their programs, warning that an overly zealous and myopic pursuit of environmental goals will precipitate an "environmental backlash" that will be the movement's undoing. The environmentalists counter with charges of "environmental blackmail," asserting that selfish interests are exploiting both the environment and the worker in the pursuit of some fast profits.

This book is not aimed at disputing or attempting to dispel these contentions. But neither is it intended to sustain them. It is not a *mea culpa* for the environmental movement—a confession of sin or an act of contrition. Yet, as the reader will find, it is not contrived to exonerate the motives and methods of environmentalism from charges that it may be indifferent or insensitive to other social issues. What is attempted is a hard, honest look at the environmental movement as it is manifested in American society today. It is an attempt to gain perspective on the environmental issue, and the movement that supports it, from the vantage of other legitimate and sometimes competing interests in today's society.

What follows is mainly the product of a three-day seminar, held by the Conservation Foundation in late 1972, on the subject, *Environmental Quality and Social Justice*. Those at the seminar represented a cross-section of social, economic, and political interests, ranging from environmentalism through inner-city activism, the social sciences, and organized labor.

Two papers included here—that by Peter Marcuse, entitled "Conservation for Whom?" (Chapter III), and that by Charles E. Little on "The Double Standard of Open Space" (Chapter VI)—were presented in abridged form at the seminar. The authors subsequently expanded them for this volume. In addition, two pieces not presented at the seminar appear in this publication. The essay by the editor on "The Coming of Age of the Environmental Movement in American Society" (Chapter II) was prepared as a kind of overview piece. Hazel Henderson's essay, "Redefining Economic Growth" (Chapter VIII), was commissioned as a synthesizing piece for that very diffuse topic—economic growth and environmental quality control.

Together, these essays provide a thoughtful and provocative inquiry into the relevance of environmentalism to other interests in society. It is pursued with a candor and forthrightness that many—especially those long associated with the movement as it has emerged from the confines of conservation to the broader realms of environmentalism—may find impertinent.

In publishing this book, the Foundation's purpose is not to confront or offend those who have worked hard over the years to stimulate the nation's awareness of the delicate and precarious balance of our natural system. Instead, what we hope to suggest is the need for the environmental movement to look at itself in the light of its recent ascendancy as a popular movement in society. Or, as Sydney Howe, the former President of the Foundation, has remarked:

> The environmental movement recently has become a very significant political force in this country. This force is beginning to show the capacity to change our ways of living by adjusting attitudes and habits. The challenge for those who operate in the environmental field is to set goals and develop procedures that make this force fully relevant to all of our people and, as such, part of a large set of forces working in some concert for the public interest.

It is in this spirit that the Foundation has undertaken publication of this volume—not as a definitive statement of the issues, but as a first, tentative step toward the public dialogue that must ensue if environmentalism is to be sustained as a legitimate force in American society.

J.N.S.

Participants

The following is a list of the persons who attended the Conservation Foundation's Conference on Environmental Quality and Social Justice in November, 1972, with their titles and affiliations at that time:

JOHN ABBOTT
Executive Secretary
California Tomorrow
San Francisco, California

CHARLES ALLEN
Director of Development and Planning
City of Gary
Gary, Indiana

PETER BORRELLI
The Sierra Club
Washington, D. C.

MRS. LEE BOTTS
Lake Michigan Federation
Chicago, Illinois

STEWART BRANDBORG
Executive Director
The Wilderness Society
Washington, D. C.

LAWRENCE BURR
General Manager
State Park Commission for City of New York
New York, New York

JAMES CANNON
Council on Economic Priorities
New York, New York

PROFESSOR CHARLES CICCHETTI
Department of Economics
University of Wisconsin
Madison, Wisconsin

PETER CUNNINGHAM
Council on Population and Environment
Rochester, New York

PAUL DAVIDOFF
Co-Director
Suburban Action Institute
White Plains, New York

ARTHUR A. DAVIS
Vice President for Operations
The Conservation Foundation
Washington, D. C.

REVEREND LEONARD DUBI
Citizen Action Program
Chicago, Illinois

WALTER GREEN
President
Black Grove, Inc.
Miami, Florida

JOHN HAMPTON
Associate
National Tenants Organization
Washington, D. C.

MRS. TERRY HERSHEY
Citizens' Environmental Coalition
Houston, Texas

SYDNEY HOWE
President
The Conservation Foundation
Washington, D. C.

MORTON ISLER
Director of Housing Studies
The Urban Institute
Washington, D. C.

CHARLES E. LITTLE
Senior Associate
The Conservation Foundation
Washington, D. C.

SAM LOVE
Coordinator
Environmental Action, Inc.
Washington, D. C.

PROFESSOR PETER MARCUSE
School of Architecture & Urban Planning
Los Angeles, California

REVEREND RICHARD NEUHAUS
Pastor
St. John the Evangelist Church
Brooklyn, New York

SENATOR RICHARD H. NEWHOUSE
Illinois State Senate
Chicago, Illinois

C. McKIM NORTON
Counsel
Regional Plan Association
New York, New York

TED PANKOWSKI, JR.
Environmental Affairs Director
Izaak Walton League of America
Arlington, Virginia

REVEREND SCOTT PARADISE
Director
Boston Industrial Mission
Boston, Massachusetts

RAFE POMERANCE
Co-Director
Urban Environmental Conference
Washington, D. C.

CARL POPE
Zero Population Growth
Washington, D. C.

WAYNE REDUS
Employment Director
Human Rights Commission of San Francisco
San Francisco, California

KEITH ROBERTS
Attorney-at-Law
McCray and Roberts
San Francisco, California

MRS. ANGELA ROONEY
National Coalition for the Transportation
    Crisis
Washington, D. C.

MS. ANN ROOSEVELT
Friends of the Earth
Washington, D. C.

BUIE SEAWELL
Assistant to Director
Rocky Mountain Center on Environment
Denver, Colorado

MRS. MARJORIE SHARP
Junior League of Chicago
Woodstock, Illinois

JAMES NOEL SMITH
Senior Associate
The Conservation Foundation
Washington, D. C.

PAUL SWATEK
The Sierra Club
Lincoln, Massachusetts

J. ROSS VINCENT
Ecology Center of Louisiana
New Orleans, Louisiana

MRS. CHARLES P. YARN
President
Save America's Vital Environment
Atlanta, Georgia

JOHN YOLTON
United Auto Workers
Detroit, Michigan

JAMES R. YOUNG
Editor, Biological Sciences
McGraw-Hill Publications
New York, New York

CHAPTER I

The Coming of Age of Environmentalism in American Society

James Noel Smith
Senior Associate
The Conservation Foundation
Washington, D. C.

IT MAY BE A PARADOX characteristic of the ebb and flow of any popular movement that, at the very time environmental principles are enjoying unprecedented public acceptance, the movement that raised them is increasingly troubled. Environmental quality has grown in the last few years into one of the two or three predominant social and political themes in American life. Those personally and professionally involved in environmentalism over the last decade or so can take some satisfaction in this event, while recognizing that it is no cause for smugness. Ecological principles, aesthetic values, and prescriptions for reform may be widely recognized and better understood, but there is little evidence that the environment itself has significantly benefited from its new popularity.

Environmentalists,* recognizing the seemingly relentless march of environmental deterioration, continue to press their views with the same stridency and from the same single-minded perspective that characterized the cause when it was much less popular.

Until recently, this may have been a necessary style, conditioned by the Damoclean nature of most environmental struggles. And, what is more, it has been a useful one. The few real victories that environmentalists

---

* The terms "environmentalism" and "environmentalist" are used here in a collective sense only to represent the general characteristics of a movement. The writer recognizes that there is nothing monolithic about the structure of the environmental movement and that it accommodates many variations of individual and attitude.

1

have achieved were not won by sweet reasonableness, but by the pluck and perseverance of a few dedicated and doughty souls. Old styles, especially those born of necessity, are not easily shed.

Unfortunately, however, this single-purpose approach is bringing environmentalists increasingly into conflict with other elements of society—especially those who do not share their values and who suspect that the real impetus for environmentalists is selfish protection of class prerogative. What is occurring is inevitable in any new social movement—a political coming of age. Although environmentalism has traditionally been characterized by its essential innocence and political naïveté, it must now be responsive to its new position as a real force in society and in political decision-making.

It is understandable and quite proper, then, that its motives should be questioned and its strategies be open to public scrutiny. What this suggests for environmentalists is a need to reassess their relative position in society and to think twice about their approach as it conflicts with competing forces interested in advancing equality of social and economic opportunity in America. Otherwise, environmentalism and social justice may be on a collision course.

The Critics of Environmentalism

To those in our society more concerned with jobs, welfare, and individual dignity in a deteriorating and increasingly inhumane urban milieu, the current public sentiment for environmental quality is looked upon with some skepticism. At best, environmentalism is seen as irrelevant. At worst, it is perceived as a deliberate attempt by a bigoted and selfish white middle-class society to perpetuate its own values and protect its own life style at the expense of the poor and the underprivileged. As Norman Faramelli, of the Boston Industrial Mission, has put it: "To the poor and the low-income families, ecology may appear to be a cop-out, a flight from social realities, and a digression from dealing with the real issues of racism and social injustice." [1] Harsh allegations, to be sure, and ones that sorely sting the environmentalists.

Most environmentalists, when they think about it, don't see themselves as socially irresponsible, or selfish, or uninterested in the social and economic well-being of any segment of the populace. Least of all do they believe they are elitists or guilty of outright racial or economic bigotry. Indeed, environmentalists are more likely to see themselves as social benefactors—defenders of all mankind against the forces of despoliation. "If we work to achieve clean air or preserve open space," they will argue, "it is a benefit to all, regardless of income or color." It is frustrating and embittering for them to have their motivations questioned. As Joseph L. Fisher, president of Resources for the Future, writes in the introduction to that

2

organization's 1972 Annual Report, environmentalists "can't understand why poor people do not share the same degree of concern for clean air and water and for nature preservation. They resent being labeled as impractical, idealistic, and blind to the real problems."

Yet critics of the environmental movement—among them black activists, blue-collar workers, and a growing regiment of academicians—insist that the movement is consciously elitist.

Some critics, in fact, have found in it elements of class warfare: those who "have" trying to impede the upward mobility and social equality of those who "have not." They detect in it a subtle, but sinister reaction to the movement of the 1960s which espoused (if it did not deliver) a democratization of privilege. To those still grasping for the brass ring of prosperity, environmentalism seems a cruel subterfuge. As urbanologist Anthony Downs puts it, "The elite's environmental deterioration is often the common man's improved standard of living." [2]

Others believe that the movement's aversion to blatant materialism and its concern over unrestrained growth masks selfish anxieties among the affluent about their own social and economic security. According to this argument, what is really bothering middle- and upper-class America is not the threat that increasing affluence poses to the environment, but the threat that arrivistes pose to middle- and upper-class values and social status. Herman Kahn, of the Hudson Institute, takes delight in pointing out that *The Limits to Growth* has enjoyed its highest U.S. sales in New York's wealthy suburban Westchester County. And Peter Passell and Leonard Ross, in their recent book, *The Retreat from Riches,* remark that the "loss of privilege is only rarely marshaled as an argument against growth. Rather, it is transformed into generalized *angst* about materialistic values, a concern for the environment, an enthusiasm for population control." [3]

Still others detect various socio-cultural and theological symbolisms in the environmental movement that contain some perverse and even frightening implications. Irving Horowitz, a sociologist at Rutgers, finds in the environmental movement not only elitism, but the vestiges of a Puritan aversion to dirt and untidiness which, in effect, cast the environmentally unanointed into the cauldron of damnation with the other unregenerate souls. "The ecological movement," he writes, "is not only middle-class in character; more, it is a kind of Protestant drive toward hygiene and cleanliness, in which every home becomes a Howard Johnson's replica; and in which cleanliness is not only next to Godliness, but often indistinguishable." [4]

It is not far from the antisepsis of "Ho-Jos" to the murky realm of biological eugenics where, to be sure, some of the more offensive tenets of the ecological movement lurk. The Reverend Richard Neuhaus, among others, has pointed out some grotesque correlations between applied ecology and the philosophical strains of Nazism. As he states elsewhere in this volume,

3

"I would suggest that the idea that nature—the presumed imperative of nature—has a role in determining public policy is classically fascist."

While Neuhaus does not accuse all environmentalists of fascism, he is alarmed by the implications of some of the movement's narrow intellectual constructs. He finds, in some of the writings and statements of Paul Ehrlich, Garrett Hardin, and Lynn White, Jr., the evocation of a "kind of social Darwinism—the application of social policies of the biological model of evolution." Taken to their logical end-points, even such seemingly benign concerns as open space and wilderness preservation, a reverence for man's place in the natural system, and, most specifically, population control, bear a strong resemblance to the cultural-political rationale for *Lebensraum*, race superiority, and genocide. Absurd, perhaps, and yet the suspicion lurks, not just in the minds of a few intellectuals, but in the rhetoric of black politics. Some black leaders see population control as just another more sophisticated technique for achieving a "final solution."

Such indictments make environmentalism increasingly vulnerable to counterattack from its natural foe, those industrial and commercial interests who would blunt the movement with any weapon at hand. Corporate PR often portrays environmentalists as selfish, short-sighted, and single-minded people who seek to force compliance with environmental-quality standards, regardless of the price it might exact on industry and the government, regardless of the threat it might carry for plant closings and social displacement. Jobs and human welfare are depicted as hanging in the balance, and environmentalists as not giving a damn. Conversely, the industrialist or businessman seizes the opportunity to describe himself as interested, foremost, in the welfare of the working man and the poor. This characterization may lack persuasiveness with the poor and the blue-collar worker, but it succeeds nonetheless in casting the environmentalists as villains. It is a tactic that has become identified as the "backlash" theme.

This theme has even resounded from the highest levels of government. Secretary of Agriculture Earl Butz—who, for a brief time in early 1973, doubled as President Nixon's super-Cabinet man for environmental affairs—warned a group of environmental writers that the activists' halcyon days were drawing to an end. "The doomsday prophets have had their say, quite convincingly," he told the writers. "They have succeeded in spawning an academic and intellectual following of those who think most answers to our troubles begin with zero economic growth, and condemning our hard-won technological leadership." It is time, the Secretary asserted, for environmentalists to stop their "harassing" actions and pull into line.[5] The same theme was sounded in 1972 by Senator Henry Jackson of Washington, as he tried to garner support from organized labor in his ill-fated bid for the Democratic Presidential nomination.

Anthropologist and environmental activist Margaret Mead spoke with some anger about backlash opportunism at a recent meeting of the Suburban

4

Action Institute in New York. She suggested the existence of a conscious plot to set environmentalists, inhabitants of the inner city, and blue-collar workers against one another. And at least some members of the Nixon Administration came to the defense of the environmentalists in this pitched battle. In mid-1973, Russell E. Train, then chairman of the President's Council on Environmental Quality, scolded the backlashers for asserting that environmental activism was mainly responsible for the major economic and industrial problems the nation faces. The blame can more accurately be attributed, he said, to lack of planning by both government and industry.[6]

The significant concern for environmentalists, however, is not that they have been maligned, but rather that the relative alienation of their movement from other social issues has made it vulnerable to effective, if unprincipled, attack. Many environmentalists now believe that the movement must undertake some soul-searching, that it must begin examining the motives and the methods of the movement, its level of social awareness, the extent of its commitment to the agenda of social justice, and the implications of its thought and action upon all levels of society.

At least a few are beginning to ask these questions: Who are we? What do we really believe in vis-à-vis social justice? Can we relate to it? Are we able, in short, to give a damn?

Who Are the Environmentalists?

What does it take to be considered an environmentalist? Can anyone —without reference to education, income, social position, religious preference, or racial characteristic—qualify? Superficially, yes. All that is needed is an abiding concern for the natural environment, some basic understanding about the interrelatedness of the natural system, and a sharpened sense of indignation toward environmental abuse. Thus, in its essential definition, environmentalism is neither exclusionary nor undemocratic. A welfare mother in Roxbury or a migrant farm worker in California has as much right to claim the title "environmentalist" as does the club woman of Upper Suburbia. Indeed, the Roxbury mother and the California field hand may have a more legitimate claim since their poverty enforces a style of life that conserves resources, rather than so wastefully expending them. But, however they might feel about the environment, they do not associate themselves socially or politically with the environmental movement—nor are they likely to.

Then who does?

A survey on the make-up of environmental groups, recently conducted for the National Center for Voluntary Action (NCVA), confirmed that the environmental movement today is largely middle- to upper-middle class and almost exclusively white. Of 1,468 individuals responding to a questionnaire, 96 per cent identified themselves as Caucasian/European. The

5

two largest occupational categories were professional (21 per cent) and housewife (24 per cent). Almost half (48 per cent) had a total family income of over $10,000, and 15 per cent had a total family income of $25,000 or more. Eighty per cent of the respondents had at least some college education; of these, 21 per cent had a college degree; 15 per cent had completed some graduate work; and 23 per cent had a graduate degree.[7]

Another survey, this time of the 140,000 members of the Sierra Club, further substantiates this demographic impression of the environmentalists. The largest occupational categories were students (19 per cent), teachers (18 per cent), and managers and executives (11 per cent). Doctors, lawyers, dentists, and other professionals made up 15 per cent of the respondents; engineers and technicians, 8 per cent; and clerical and blue-collar workers, a scant 7 per cent.[8]

By way of contrast, only ten per cent of all American families clear $13,000 or more after taxes. The average take-home pay of the American worker was about $110 a week—barely enough to get by on. The fact is that most Americans do not make that much money. As the Brookings Institution's most recent assessment of the federal budget points out, "Many people are surprised when they learn where they stand in the (nation's) income distribution." An annual family income of $17,513 or more places one in the top 20 per cent, while $7,600 or more puts a single person in that category.[9]

On the other hand, even where the statistics on poverty in the U.S. show progress during the decade of the '60s in reducing the total number of poor in the U.S., there are still 26.5 million people classified as existing in a state of poverty and deprivation in our society—or approximately 12 per cent of the population.*

Thus, considering the vast numbers in the U.S. still poor and the much larger number of Americans on the twilight edge of poverty (another 36.5 million), the environmental rhetoric about the ecological insult of the "affluent society" can look either silly or grim, depending on one's perspective. According to some, such as Teamsters' Union lawyer Nicholas King, the "affluent society" is nonexistent: "It's a myth perpetuated by the ruling class."[10]

Few environmentalists look upon themselves as part of a "ruling class," but there is little question that they are part of a small, relatively affluent minority which wields social and political influence disproportionate to

---

* There is good evidence that the real amount of poverty in the U.S. is substantially higher. Even though absolute income has increased for millions of American families originally classified in the poverty category, increases in the cost of living and their deprivation relative to the rest of society keep them still poor and deprived. According to an April 9, 1973, article in the *Washington Post* ("A Passion for Equality" by William Greider and Nick Kotz), Herman Miller, an expert in income equality, believes that if the income figures were made to accurately reflect the cost of living, the results would put 40 million people in the poverty category—the same number that was there ten years before the War on Poverty got underway.

their absolute number. Their incomes, education, and occupational patterns place them securely in that small upper stratum of American society which, most social scientists concede, determines the social, cultural, and political rules of the game in America.

Where Are Their Heads?

If environmentalists are indeed part of a social and economic elite, the next thing to determine is: Where are their heads and their hearts? What is their agenda? How—and this is a crucial question—do they use their position of influence in society to affect policy and program? Not surprisingly, the two surveys cited above show that the average environmentalist has his heart in the hinterland and his head, if not buried, at least turned from the unpleasant business of human survival in urban America.

In the NCVA survey of environmental organizations, 45 per cent of the respondents listed their organization's priority interest as wilderness or natural-area preservation. Wildlife protection, water-quality control, land-use planning and control, and outdoor recreation all came close behind. Such urban-associated issues as sanitation, rat and pest control, and noise pollution came in at the very bottom of the priority list.

Generally, the same was true in the survey of the Sierra Club membership. In answer to the question, "Should the Club concern itself with the conservation problems of such special groups as the urban poor and ethnic minorities?," the reaction was heavily negative. According to the Club's survey:

> About 40 percent strongly disagreed with such a proposal, while 15 percent strongly agreed. But the younger the member, the less he opposed such involvement. Although 58 percent of all members either strongly or "somewhat" opposed such involvement, only 46 percent of those under 35 were opposed, and only 43 percent of those under 24. Members from households whose main wage earners were managers or executives tended to be more opposed to such involvement, while members from households whose main wage earners were students, clerical or blue-collar workers or "other professionals" were less opposed.[11]

These two surveys, though not a comprehensive profile of all sectors of the environmental movement, provide a fairly accurate portrait of the kind of agenda most environmentalists push. It can be argued, of course, that environmental organizations are not monolithic structures, controlling the heads and hearts of their memberships; that there is nothing to prevent an individual member of the Sierra Club or the Wilderness Society from belonging, as many of them surely do, to organizations devoted to objectives of advancing civil rights, expanding health services to the poor, or other concerns of the social sector. "When I want wilderness preservation," the argument goes, "I join a wilderness group. When I want civil rights, I support the NAACP."

In terms of operational strategies, the argument is essentially valid, but it is indicative of a kind of categorical myopia that pervades the environmental movement and reveals, perhaps, its most critical fault—the inability of the movement to see itself in respect to the larger social system, and to accommodate its own agenda to other competing social priorities.

Environmentalists are insisting on—and getting—important new legislation that can produce sweeping changes in an economic system based on a correlation between consumer-product consumption and an upwardly mobile work force. The campaign for pollution control, with its emphasis on the internalization of control expenses as part of the production cost, is a good example. These costs will show up as higher prices, placing the greater burden on the poor, who have less discretionary income to absorb price increases. Land-use controls, and their tendency to drive up the cost of housing, work the same kind of displacements on the poor and low-income family by making low-cost housing even scarcer than it is. The short-term effects of such environmental protection measures can, therefore, be fundamentally disruptive to the entire industrial and commercial system. For even if higher prices did not seriously affect sales, the absorption of new pollution-control costs would produce an inevitable profit-lag at the bottom line. If such a lag widely obtains, severe economic dislocations involving lay-offs can occur.

In view of such a complexity of cause and effect, environmentalists have an obligation to understand the social and economic implications of their action agenda. As Lee Rainwater cautions, "If those who want to solve problems understand too little about how people in this society live and what they want out of life, then they run the risk of suggesting solutions that are either irrelevant or anathema to their countrymen." [12]

Herman Kahn believes that this is indeed the case with regard to the upper middle class in America's post-industrial society. Kahn thinks that there is an increasing social and cultural alienation of the upper middle class from the rest of America. "In the past ten years," he tells us, "a large per cent of them (the upper middle class) lost all touch with reality, the realities of American politics and American issues." [13] Thus, according to Kahn, the peculiar social myopia of environmentalists could be described as merely a symptom of a pathological failure of our upper middle class society—comparable, he tells us, to the failure of that same class in the Greek city-state society.

Another fundamental, if less socially dynamic, explanation for the inability of environmentalists to transcend the narrow confines of their agenda and see their interest in the context of a total social system might be found in a basic philosophical approach that, put quite simply, is not man-oriented. While environmentalists frequently possess some profound insights into the interdependent relationship of man to his natural environment, it does not automatically follow that such insightfulness is applied to man in his social and political contexts.

"Environmentalism, so far, has not been concerned with forging a compatible accommodation between man in nature and man as a social and political animal. Indeed, much environmental thinking is distrustful of the essential nature of man."

The philosophical roots of the environmental movement, such as they are, are found almost exclusively in the contemplation of man's relationship to nature. The emphasis has been on the interdependencies of the ecosystem, with man portrayed as one small, albeit influential, part. Understandably, perhaps, such emphasis has tended to ignore man as a social or political being. While environmentalism may, in some of its aspects, reflect the 18th-century romanticism of a Jean-Jacques Rousseau and belief in the fundamental nobility of man in a natural state, Rousseau and the other romanticists also perceived man as fundamentally perfectible, and the establishment of a balance between the individual's self-interest and his social and political responsibilities (the "social contract") as essential.

Environmentalism, so far, has not been concerned with forging a compatible accommodation between man in nature and man as a social and political animal. Indeed, much environmental thinking is distrustful of the essential nature of man. Most recent environmental legislation is based upon the thesis that unless restricted and prohibited by threat of fine, imprisonment, or social sanction, man will lay waste the natural landscape and defile his own habitat. It could be argued, then, that instead of being essentially romantic, environmental thought is really much closer to classic conservatism in its distrust of human nature and its adherence to a hierarchical ordering of things, both in the natural and the social system.

Do They "Give A Damn"?

To generalize is to be an idiot, as William Blake warned, but one is hard put to make a case that the strains of egalitarianism run deep in environmentalism. One need not know the environmental movement well to recognize that one of its major themes is, "Let's save the place for those who understand and value it as we do," which frequently is decoded into, "Let's keep 'those other people' out."

The exclusionary theme is being played out on practically every front of environmental action today, in the wilderness and the suburbs alike. But wherever it occurs, the impulse is basically the same: protection of a value system that sustains or enhances a place of privilege from the incursions of those outside forces that can be expected to diminish the value of the protected area for its present and future users.

The person who enjoys wandering through some favorite glen or glade can hardly be expected to delight in the prospect that such an area is about to be overrun by the masses. He senses immediately, and no doubt accurately, that his own experience will be diminished—and diminished, moreover, by those who lack the sophistication, the learning, and, possibly, the basic intelligence to recognize and share the aesthetic values he finds in untrammeled nature.

This protective instinct of the woods-walker can be applied to entire suburban communities. Typically, such communities react negatively to development proposals that will greatly alter the character of the area in which they live. They see such proposals primarily as threats—an infringement upon open space, an impaction of public facilities and services, an overloading of the financial capabilities of local government.

Proposals for suburban development that contain some modest provisions of housing for the poor or jobs for the unemployed frequently receive an unwelcome reception from the community. This is often branded as "racism." But it is questionable whether this is an accurate characterization of the motivational forces behind such resistance. Such resistance may well come not so much from racial intolerance as from a complex of self-protective instincts that define the proposed change as a threat to social, economic, and environmental well-being. Environmental protectionism may lead to inferences of racism, but to brand such devices as large-lot zoning, growth-control strategies, and open-space land preservation as evidence of racial feeling misses the point and deflects the issue. Such simplifications seem to assume that discrimination is still mainly attitudinal; that all that is required is for everybody to "be nice."

But as the realities of the '70s displace the euphoria of the early '60s, we are coming to the painful recognition that the inequities of the generations of discriminatory treatment are not simply dispelled by a change in public attitude. "Much of what is perceived as the effect of presently existing white prejudice," Edward C. Banfield tells us, "is, in fact, largely or even entirely the effect of factors that owe their existence to prejudice *in the past*." [14] Or, as Rainwater points out, the reason our social and political models for bringing about racial equality in America have met with so much frustration is the ". . . discovery of how tenaciously interconnected inequalities are so that it becomes almost impossible to produce equality of opportunity except in a situation in which there is, in fact, also equality of result." [15] This goes to the very core of the question of equality of social and economic opportunity, an issue which appears to be emerging as one of the dominant intellectual and even political issues of the decade, and one which must be taken seriously by the environmental movement.

Daniel Bell calls the question—equality of opportunity versus equality of result—"the central value problem of the post-industrial society." In an important essay, he explains why this question is so enormous:

> . . . What is at stake today is the redefinition of equality. A principle which was the weapon for changing a vast social system, the principle of equality of opportunity, is now seen as leading to a new hierarchy, and the current demand is that the "just precedence" of society, in Locke's phrase, requires the reduction of all inequality, or the creation of *equality of result*—in income, status, and power—for all men in society.[16]

If one accepts this proposition—which, incidentally, Bell does not—one arrives rather quickly at the question of the redistribution of wealth. In other words, if access to opportunity is cut off by a self-enforcing hierarchical social system, it is often suggested that the most expedient way to rebalance the system is to forcibly redistribute the spoils. A 1973 series in the *Washington Post,* entitled "A Passion for Equity," put the question in these pragmatic terms:

> . . . Is the country prepared to redistribute income, jobs and housing in a way that will produce "equality of results" sooner? Or is the government's commitment merely to provide "equality of opportunity" consistent with the traditional competition for jobs and income? The questions of "opportunity" and "results" overlap because it is hard to persuade the victim of discrimination that he enjoys "equal opportunity" when he still cannot see anything resembling equal results.[17]

One of the consequences of the emergence of the equality issue into the arena of public debate has been to severely shake our conventional faith in the efficacy of Keynesian economic theory and liberal political programs. There is a growing skepticism in the capacity of traditional Keynesian economic formulas for an ever-expanding economy to provide new opportunities for upward mobility to poorer members of society. In the same way, there is a growing disenchantment with the political proposition, born of the social welfare programs of the New Deal in the 1930s and nurtured by liberal political policy through the '50s and the '60s, that a beneficent government can effectively increase the opportunity quotient with programs aimed at giving the poor or the disadvantaged an upward boost. We now know that during the period of our nation's greatest economic growth (the end of World War II to the present), there has been little significant change in the distributive patterns of wealth in American society. Economists at the Brookings Institution note that 20 per cent of the families at the top of the income scale receive about 42 per cent of all family income, while the 20 per cent at the bottom receive less than six per cent. "Moreover," they point out, "these percentages have remained virtually unchanged since World War II." [18] Regressive policies of taxation, ample loopholes and

---

"The other choice is for environmentalists to move toward social accommodation by helping design social policy that incorporates environmental precepts and ecological understandings with an honest concern for a more equitable allocation of resources and distribution of income and power in American society."

---

other public programs of preferential treatment have worked to enforce inequitable distribution of wealth, as well as environmental degradation.

We are beginning to recognize, too, that many of our public programs—spawned by a liberal dedication to utilizing the public sector to help equalize opportunity—have ended up primarily as subsidies to the income and life styles of middle-class America, and too often with disastrous effects on the environments of the urban poor. After some twenty years of presumably progressive public programs for health insurance, aid to colleges and universities, federal housing and public works, Passell and Ross suggest that their effect has been "simply (to) funnel money to the middle class." They go on to explain:

> ... Federal transportation subsidies overwhelmingly aid the automobile, not the subway; farm programs sustain the squire, not the serf; urban renewal assuages the middle classes and dispossesses the poor. Federal housing programs confer twenty times as much benefit on a family earning $50,000 as on one earning $5000. National health-insurance proposals would multiply the burden of the payroll tax, heavily concentrated on the working poor.[19]

Environmentalism is in the vortex of this inequality debate for two reasons. First, as pointed out earlier, environmentalists are so well ensconced in the hierarchical structure that their efforts in behalf of environmental quality will invariably be seen as essentially self-protective by those

12

elements of society less well-positioned in the system. Secondly, the environmentalists' concern with the environmental impacts of rampant economic growth and development has caused them to question the efficacy of Keynesian formulas and to begin to visualize the possibilities of a "no-growth" or "steady-state" economy which, in its articulation, raises questions of equality and distribution.

Situated in the middle of this gathering storm, the environmentalists have a choice. They can—and very well might—choose to ignore the whole business: to make a deliberate determination to take the environmental movement out of the equality debate altogether. Passell and Ross point out, quite accurately, that little is said in the standard environmental polemic about income distribution.[20] Most environmentalists are not comfortable with the topic of income maldistribution, although Barry Commoner is an exception. In his book *The Closing Circle*, Commoner analyzes the distribution question in the context of total world production and resources exploitation, pointing out that the capital-intensive methods of the rich nations have been built on the backs of the poorer nations through an effective process of economic colonization. Moreover, Commoner points out, these economic production processes are not only socially exploitative, but environmentally exploitative as well—which causes him to formulate the maxim, "ecological sanity now requires social justice."[21]

A few other environmentalist efforts, such as Hazel Henderson's organized attempt to turn the economics profession toward a more public-interest orientation, recognize the critical need for applying the Commoner maxim to the domestic economic-political system. As Irving Horowitz suggests, ". . . the physical improvement of the quality of life will mean precious little if it assists only the precious few. . . . The ecology movement, for its own survival, must become more linked to economic problems and less to ideological posturing."[22] If it tries to exist outside the mainstream of economic and political thought, it will be in real danger of losing its relevance as a social movement and a good deal of its following as well—ending up, as Lee Rainwater suggests it may, as "merely another amusement for the alienated intellectual elite."[23]

The other choice is for environmentalists to move toward social accommodation by helping design social policy that incorporates environmental precepts and ecological understandings with an honest concern for a more equitable allocation of resources and distribution of income and power in American society.

Toward Social Accommodation

It is probably a fair speculation that the current national drift away from social and political idealism is a passing anomaly born of disappointment and frustration, rather than a permanent retrenchment. Even though

13

they may not understand the causes and syndromes of poverty, most members of middle-class suburban society, where the largest share of those who identify with environmentalism are found, recognize the sheer impracticality of isolation from the pathologies of the inner city. Much of the impetus for the War on Poverty, as Lee Rainwater has pointed out, stemmed from a clear realization that poverty could be a threat to the comfort and security of the more affluent in America, if only because it makes for "a threatening and unattractive social milieu." [24]

Today, the very presence of public disillusionment over the intractable nature of this unattractive milieu suggests that the impulse for reform may be undimmed and that America is about to return from its present drift into social nihilism and readdress itself to the search for solutions. It is inconceivable to suppose that nearly two centuries of progress in the development of humanitarian principles can be permanently wiped out by momentary frustrations.

If, then, it is correct to assume that American society, in general, will move increasingly toward social accommodation, the environmental movement has a real opportunity to help formulate and influence national policies and strategies in this direction. Where and how should it begin?

Certainly, it should start by recognizing the needs of other elements of society and assessing the impact and the implications of environmental actions upon them. Environmentalists must look at such things as the obvious relationship of environmental quality and land-use controls to overall economic stability and to the social continuity of a community. The efforts toward growth limitation or a slow-down have to be made with a full understanding of economic processes and impacts on employment.

Just as important, but more difficult to come to grips with, environmentalists have to understand that the priorities of their own agenda must be measured against other social needs. Thus, in the usual circumstance of strained municipal budgets, water-pollution control facilities simply may not rank as high on the list of human needs in the community as health services or housing.

Finally, environmentalists must make the linkages between their traditional concern for the preservation of the natural landscape and the ecological health of the urban environment. Hunger, malnutrition, poor health, and premature death—induced by poisons from lead, air pollution, rats, and other disease-carrying rodents—are also indicative of America's unbalanced ecology.

Although "volunteerism" is currently in vogue, at least in official circles, real solutions to the questions of social and economic equity will come about only through the interaction of the national economic and political system, which means, of course, corrective action on the part of government. To the extent that environmentalists have an influence upon the policies and programs of government, they have a responsibility to assure that they

14

do not inadvertently advance policies (or support politicians) hostile to the needs of the urban poor, or commandeer resources that are needed for urban survival.

By and large, environmentalists have done a good job of calling public attention to the "constraints imposed by ecology"—and that is about where the movement stands today. It has attracted the public and taught it, however tentatively, a few of the basic precepts of ecology.

Overall, however, environmentalism will have its greatest positive impact in the contribution it can make toward the design of long-range perspectives that transcend narrow constraints of social justice and environmental quality. It should develop new synthesizing "visions," as Peter Borrelli calls them, of a future in which social justice and environmental quality are indistinguishable. Such visions should be, in the words of the Yale planner, Christopher Tunnard, ". . . born of the constraints imposed by ecology and the liberation afforded by the adoption of coherent social policies."[25] It is here that the environmental community can exert real leadership. The climate, moreover, is propitious.

NOTES TO CHAPTER ONE

1. Norman Faramelli, "Economic Growth, Social Justice and Ecology." Address at Northern Illinois University, De Kalb, Illinois. May 5, 1972.

2. Anthony Downs, "Up and Down with Ecology," *The Public Interest*, Summer, 1972, p. 44.

3. Peter Passell and Leonard Ross, *The Retreat from Riches*. Viking Press, 1973, p. 9.

4. Irving L. Horowitz, "The Environmental Cleavage," *Environmental Quality and Social Responsibility*, University of Wisconsin-Green Bay, 1972, p. 126.

5. Earl Butz, "Facing our Environmental Destiny." Address to Environmental Writers Association of America. Washington, D. C. February 6, 1973.

6. Russell E. Train, "Remarks before the American Power Conference. Chicago, Illinois. May 8, 1973.

7. Clem L. Zinger *et al.*, *Environmental Volunteers in America*, National Center for Voluntary Action, Washington, D. C., 1973, pp. 5-23.

8. Don Coombs, "The Club Looks at Itself," *Sierra Club Bulletin*, July-August, 1972.

9. Charles L. Schultze *et al.*, *Setting National Priorities: the 1974 Budget*, Brookings Institution, Washington, D. C., 1973, p. 41.

10. William Greider and Nick Kotz, "A Passion for Equality," *Washington Post*, April 9, 1973.

11. Coombs, *op. cit.*

12. Lee Rainwater, "The Urban Social Environment," *Environmental Quality and Social Justice, op. cit.*, p. 110.

13. Stephen Isaacs, "Misunderstanding America," interview with Herman Kahn, *Washington Post*, July 1, 1973.

14. Edward C. Banfield, "A Critical View of the Urban Crisis," *The Annals of the American Academy of Political and Social Science*, January, 1973, p. 12.

15. Rainwater, *op. cit.*, p. 103.

16. Daniel Bell, "On Meritocracy and Equality," *The Public Interest*, Fall, 1972, p. 40.

17. Greider and Kotz, *op. cit.*

18. Schultze *et al.*, *op. cit.*, p. 41.

19. Passell and Ross, *op. cit.*, p. 14.

20. Passell and Ross, *op. cit.*, p. 45.

21. Barry Commoner, *The Closing Circle*, Alfred A. Knopf, New York, N. Y., 1971.

22. Horowitz, *op. cit.*, p. 131.

23. Rainwater, *op. cit.*, p. 110.

24. *Ibid.*, p. 110.

25. Christopher Tunnard, "The Planning Syndrome in Western Culture," *The Annals of the American Academy of Political and Social Science*, January, 1973, p. 103.

CHAPTER II

Conservation for Whom?

Peter Marcuse
Department of Architecture and Urban Planning
University of California at Los Angeles

UNCHARITABLY, IT MIGHT BE SAID that the conservation movement has come to a concern for inner-city problems late in life, reluctantly, and only under the pressure of outside circumstances.

Such a statement would of course be grossly unfair to many individuals and many organizations in the environmental movement; no such consistent pattern can be attributed to a movement that is as heterogeneous as is conservation.* Yet there is enough truth to it to make it worth exploring; indeed, it will be argued here that there is a strong tendency within the conservation movement to treat social concerns in an offhand and third-class way, a tendency which is neither accidental nor the result of short-sightedness, but which arises out of the same source as much of the conservation movement itself.

In a nutshell, the argument presented here is this: Policies giving priority to environmental concerns frequently clash with those directed at inner-city concerns. The treatment of these clashes by the conservation movement is generally superficial and misleading: their existence is either denied in some euphoric statement of global goals, or they are attributed to local complexities and misunderstandings that "better communications" could correct. But the frequent clash of environmental and social-develop-

---

* Certain terms are used in this paper in a schematic sense: "the conservation movement" should, to be correct in each case, be "many of the individuals and organizations most active in the support of conservation causes in the U.S."; "inner-city problems" include problems of poverty, discrimination, unemployment, poor housing, inadequate education, and kindred problems (including environmental quality as one, but only one, and many of which are to be found outside of as well as inside inner-city areas); the "inner-city movement" is only conceptually a single movement, and its definition would need to employ all the qualifiers attached to "conservation movement" above; "social concerns" or "inner-city concerns" means concerns with inner-city problems in terms of the priorities of those affected most directly by them, and "social development policies" means policies explicitly directed towards those priorities.

ment policies is not accidental. The difficulty is not one of sophistication of formulation, or courtesy in conduct, but of clash of group interests. Conservationists by and large are middle- or upper-class white suburbanites, members of that very section of society that has been the main beneficiary of the activities that have created much of the present environmental pollution. Their immediate personal objective is often simply escapist—an attempt to protect the privileged lifestyles they now have, and isolate themselves personally from the effects of pollution. This ability to escape personally is now threatened by the increasing geographic extent or severity of pollution. On the other hand, inner-city residents have always lived with pollution. They have more immediate concerns, unrelated to the problems environmentalists are worried about. Each could today benefit politically by an alliance with the other, but no immediate identity of interest exists on which to base such an alliance. If the conservation movement is interested in forming a firm alliance with the inner-city movement, these strategies are open to it: bridge-building, log-rolling, or social change. All but the first require changes in the prevailing conservationist philosophy and understanding, as well as improvements in strategy or tactics. Whether these will come about or not remains to be seen.

Such an argument borders dangerously on the glittering generality on the one side and the not-so-glittering *ad hominem* argument on the other, and should not be made without substantial evidence. The very publication of this volume by the Conservation Foundation, and the holding of the conference on which it is based, indicates the existence of countervailing trends. The good faith and integrity of the commitment to social justice of many leaders and members of the "conservation movement" is beyond question. It is not the purpose of this paper to cast doubt on that commitment, or to disparage those countervailing trends, but, rather, to show the depth of the conflicts they face and attempt to analyze their causes. Even if it is painful, diagnosis must precede prescription. Whether the diagnosis presented here is correct or not, there is enough evidence to show that it must be dealt with honestly in the common search for the best cure to the major problems of environmental degradation and social justice.

Where Interests Clash

Let us start by looking at the evidence derived from actual cases of clash or concord of interest between conservation and inner-city causes. One case is often adduced where the two blend neatly: the Sierra Club and the NAACP join in seeking to block construction of a highway in Oakland, California, the one opposing because of environmental consequences, the other because of threatened destruction of low-rent housing.[1] The same alliance comes about in opposition to the Three Sisters Bridge across the Potomac in Washington, D. C., and to freeway expansion and insensitive transportation planning in Boston.

Such cases are very appealing, and indeed opposition to the highway lobby probably is one of those areas where the two interests do, in fact, coincide most frequently. Yet, even in the highway cases, the unity is often more in opposing a common enemy than in supporting common alternatives. Where the environmental movement clearly comes down on the side of such mass-transit systems as Bay Area Rapid Transit (BART), there is serious room for doubt that inner-city interests are well served. The negative environmental impacts of BART's tracks crossing the inner-city areas of Oakland, to serve the needs of the well-to-do suburbanites of Fremont, may make BART a commuter's dream but an inner-city nightmare.[2] Be that as it may, a quick review of just a few of the issues on which conservation and inner-city concerns seem to differ is instructive:

- "Higher prices which result from pollution control will force the costs to be 'borne disproportionately by those with lower incomes because they spend a larger percentage of their incomes on such products.' "[3] The Council on Environmental Quality points out that if the estimated cost of pollution-control devices on cars is $500, it will mean a 25% increase in the cost of a $2500 car, but only a 10% increase in the price of a $5,000 car, a regressive effect which hits even harder at the owners of older used cars.

- Environmental-impact statements are now required of many projects, including low-income federally assisted housing. They provide a large quantity of data on the impact of such a project on the physical environment. But, typically, they do not take into account the differential needs of those to be benefited by each project; in other words, a luxury condominium and a public housing project, built to the identical specifications, may be evaluated identically, if, indeed, the public housing is not rated lower because of its potentially "detrimental" effect on the neighborhood. What is needed is a type of "Reverse Impact Statement" that would also take into account the nature of the present environment of those the project is designed to serve.[4] But this is not presently being contemplated.

- California's recent coastal conservation referendum, adopted by the state's voters in 1972, is likewise formally "neutral" as to the total social benefit that may or may not be derived from a particular project. Only consequences within the coastal zone are to be considered, not the net impact elsewhere. A parking structure for an exclusive resort hotel is evaluated no differently from one for a badly needed public beach. At least one Section 236 lower-income project has already been blocked because of the referendum.

- In Suffolk County, New York, a lawsuit brought by environmental groups challenged the zoning ordinance of Suffolk County because it allegedly permitted excessive development at the expense of the environment. The plaintiffs are asking that there be prepared, instead, an "environmentally oriented, ecologically protected, sociologically responsible, economically feasible, administratively sound and politically practical ordinance." [5] Until that day arrives, they request that no building permits be issued by the county. It may take a little time to prepare an ordinance meeting these specifications. In the meantime, the housing supply in Suffolk County cannot be increased, regardless of inner-city needs.

• Next door, in Nassau County, the NAACP has brought a lawsuit, challenging the very large-lot zoning that many conservationists support, on the grounds that, under the guise of ecology, the Town of Oyster Bay is keeping out blacks.[6]

• San Antonio Ranch, outside San Antonio, Texas, is proposing a new town to be federally assisted under the Housing Act of 1968. The Sierra Club and other environmental groups have brought an injunction action to halt construction. Thirty to forty per cent of residences in San Antonio Ranch are designed for low- or moderate-income families. The problem is that it is apparently sitting on one of the aquifers that feed into San Antonio and will create some problems for the city, where the low-income population is nowhere near thirty to forty per cent. Who should pay for the resolution of that problem? It may have a simple technical answer, but the potential conflict is clear.[7]

• Hawaii and Vermont have passed, and other states are considering, state-level land-use and environmental-protection laws which have the net effect of increasing the cost of housing; in Hawaii and Vermont, estimates are that there is an additional cost of $500 per unit just to comply with the paperwork required under these laws.[8]

• The San Francisco Bay fill issue brought some rather hostile confrontations between the NAACP in Oakland and the Save the Bay Committee because the Bay areas of Oakland have been developed for heavy industrial use. These areas employ a large number of low-income workers and house a lot of low-income families. The interest in stimulating employment, on the part of the black community in Oakland, is much higher than their interest in promoting sound yachting or pleasanter-appearing water in San Francisco Bay, and Bay fill seems a perfectly legitimate means to them of pursuing that interest.

• A trans-Sierra power line was tentatively proposed to decrease the cost of electric power in the Bay area, but the threat of unsightly transmission lines quickly killed the idea.

• In Chicago, a proposal to use Garfield Park as the site for a school to serve a low-income population was opposed by conservation-oriented groups. Clearly, both sides would prefer not to build schools in parks, but sometimes a hard choice has to be made, and inner-city and conservation interests may well conflict.

• The clash of interests on construction of the SST is well known; it involves generally the same polarization as develops from the no-growth campaigns.

20

• The general movement to limit growth by preventing further residential construction has provoked some of the most bitter direct confrontations. In Boulder, Colorado; Livermore, California; Ramapo, New Jersey; Suffolk County, New York; and in countless other areas, the efforts of conservation-oriented groups to prevent "environmental degradation" by a variety of ordinances, building or zoning restrictions, moratoria on water or sewer hookups, etc., have evoked strong opposition from blue-collar workers, as well as lower-income and minority groups.

• The Gateway West controversy (the Golden Gate National Recreational Area proposal) is written up in illuminating detail in the Conservation Foundation's *National Parks for the Future*.[9] The original proposal of the National Park Service had a serious urban orientation: it offered recreational resources readily accessible to the low-income residents of San Francisco's "inner city." Conservationist groups supporting it suggested—undoubtedly in all good faith—that it be expanded to include high-income, low-density and non-urban parts of Marin County. The net result is that the Marin County expansion was approved and the original urban section reduced. Between the two, inner-city residents would undoubtedly have preferred the opposite result.

• At the proposed Tocks Island reservoir is the Delaware Water Gap National Recreation Area, the largest natural area feasible for major recreational development between New York City and Philadelphia. Conservation groups have been strong advocates of reducing the plans of the National Park Service from a development to serve 10 million people a year to one that would serve 2.5 million per year, in the name of protection of environmental values. Who are the 7.5 million who aren't going to use it because of that change?

• Implicit conflicts over budget priorities occur every year and at every level of government; revenue-sharing will shift some of the controversy temporarily to the local level. But as long as resources are limited, a given budget can handle only so much open-space acquisition and so much low-income housing; less of one can mean more of another. Or, as Norman Faramelli has more graphically pointed out, "in the ecology movement, the recycling of trash is rightly seen as an important function . . . The ghetto resident, however, has a prior problem . . . will the trash be collected in the first place?"[10]

• Several national land-use planning bills are now pending in Congress, best known of which is Senator Jackson's. They are conservation-oriented. The problem they deal with is the protection of major natural-resource land from an extension of the present pattern of urban sprawl and the gobbling up of open space by subdivisions. The problem they do not deal with is the provision of housing, and the land required for it and its related facilities, for those who now and in the future will continue to dwell in overcrowded slums in the inner city. As Fred Hayes has pointed out, "a development policy is as important as a land-use policy, and, in fact, it is critical to a land-use policy." [11] Hayes politely says the bills are not "bad, merely incomplete and partial," suggesting the possibility that land-use controls for the environmentally concerned could be smoothly coupled with the development planning needed by inner-city residents. Perhaps; but the issue surrounding even simple questions, such as whether the Department of the Interior (or EPA) or the Department of Housing and Urban Development should be the administering agency, suggests otherwise.

No good purpose would be served by multiplying the examples of conflict between conservation and inner-city concerns further. The essential point is that these concerns do very frequently clash, and when they do, conservationists put their specific concern first. Nor does the trend, at least on the public level, seem to be changing. [12] To the contrary, if the annual reports of the Council on Environmental Quality are any indication, the interest of the federal conservation establishment is shifting *away from* concern with inner-city problems.

In the Second Annual Report of the CEQ, there is a section on inner-city environment. It deals with lead poisoning, factory gases, and such things.* It's a small chapter, but it has a great deal of information in it on the day-to-day environmental problems of working people and inner-city residents.

In CEQ's Third Annual Report, these items are not pursued. There is no discussion of inner-city problems. There is no discussion of the differential effect on different groups of the environmental-protection movement. There is a chapter, under "Costs of Pollution Control," to which one might turn in expectation of a discussion of *who* is going to pay. But the only issue raised is whether the oil companies or Ford pay initially, what the differential effect of various proposals will be among the industries affected, and how the universal costs will get passed on to the consumers. The distributional effect by income or ethnic group is never so much as mentioned. The previous year's report had at least acknowledged the problem. [13]

So there is much evidence of the existence of conflict between conservation and inner-city priorities and programs. Are these conflicts simply the fortuitous and unhappy results of the immaturity or lack of sophistication of the conservation and/or the inner-city movements, which a kinder tomorrow may turn into a harmonious and mutually reinforcing relationship? Or is there reason to believe that these conflicts are not mere coincidences, but indicative of longer-term differences in the nature, interests, and objectives of the two movements?

---

* In a survey of the priority interests of leaders of the conservation movement reported on by James Noel Smith in the previous chapter of this volume, neither factory safety nor any other condition of employment appeared.

22

An examination of the social and economic character of the inner-city and conservation movements, and the historical origin of the present wave of conservation interest, may help in answering this question.

Tracing the Roots of the Movement

The roots of the "inner-city movement" are not hard to find. Essentially, they lie in two patterns: the centuries-old pattern of, first, slavery; then, discrimination and segregation that has confronted black people in America and, to a different extent, other racial and national minorities; and the more recent pattern of industrialization, rapid urban growth, unequal distribution of income, unemployment, and inadequate quality of public services that is a characteristic of most metropolitan areas in the U.S. today. As a result, the inner-city movement can be readily characterized in social, economic, and ethnic terms: it is lower-class, poor, and largely minority.

Can the conservation movement be similarly categorized in terms of *its* social, economic, or ethnic characteristics? I think so. Take a look at the composition of the board of directors of any of the major national conservation organizations. Look at the local memberships of the active conservation groups. Look at the mailing lists of their magazines. These are, of course, crude indicators, and the argument is indeed *ad hominem*, but it is not unfair. And personal knowledge and experience need not, after all, be entirely disregarded in discussions such as this: indeed, are not most of those whom we know to be active in the conversation movement basically middle- or upper-class, moderately or quite well-off, white, and native-born?

While there have been no comprehensive formal studies of the composition of conservationist boards or membership rolls of which I am aware,[14] there have been a number of sociological studies of users of certain recreational facilities that might correlate highly with conservation interests: wilderness use, backpacking, hiking, bird-watching, fishing, and hunting. With the partial exception of the last two activities, the findings are always that the sociological characteristics of those involved in these activities is significantly skewed toward those who are upper-income, professional and managerial, college-educated, white, and heads of household.

A few figures will suffice:

• According to the 1965 Survey of Outdoor Recreation Activities, "ten per cent of the white population went camping during the summer. The per cent of campers who were Negro and other races was too small to be significant." [15]

• The ORRRC National Recreation Survey found that "among employed persons 14 years of age and over, only the professional, technical and the white-collar group participate to any appreciable extent (in hiking)." [16]

• Visits to National and State parks and recreation areas ran, according to another ORRRC study, about five times as high for families with incomes over $7,500 as it did for those under $3,000.[17]

• According to a 1970 Survey of Outdoor Recreation Activities, whites spent 424,976,000 "recreation days" in bird watching during that year, compared to 7,539,000 for "Negro and other."[18] The survey also found that 3.1 per cent of the people in the United States with only an elementary education participated in bird watching, whereas 9.5 per cent of those with four years of college engaged in that activity.[19] For nature walks, the comparable figures were 9.4 per cent and 28 per cent.[20]

• Figures in the same report show that 44.6 per cent of those with annual incomes under $1,000 participated in some kind of outdoor recreation activity in 1970. This percentage rises steadily with each level of income, to a peak of 89.8 per cent for those with annual incomes of $25,000 or more. As for those who did not participate in *any* outdoor recreation activity at all, the report said that 21.8% of the whites were non-participants, compared with 40.4% for minorities. The top occupational categories in percentage of participants were professional and technical personnel, managers, officials, and proprietors; the bottom categories were farm laborers and foremen, and private household workers.[21]

• Summarizing a National Park Service study of Parks users, Doris Y. Wilkinson points out that "the higher the educational status, the more

---

"The split lifestyle — in which the working day is spent in pollution- and congestion-creating activity in the city, and the evening, week-end, and vacation is spent far removed from pollution and congestion — is no longer feasible except for a very small minority."

---

likely one is to be a user," and makes the same comment with regard to incomes and whites as opposed to non-whites.[22] Other studies come to a similar conclusion.[23] A general correlation between the composition of participants in these types of activities and the composition of the participants in the conservation movement may be plausibly assumed.

Nor is it an historical accident that socio-economic characteristics of the conservation movement are essentially middle- or upper-class, moderately or quite well-off, and white. A careful and analytic history of the conservation movement in the United States, from a socio-economic point of view, has yet to be written. If it were, the setting in which it would be placed might look somewhat as follows:

Concern for the quality of the physical environment is hardly a recent development. Those able to afford a decent home in a suitable neighborhood and environment have long been able to find such a home. With the development of modern industrial economy and the accompanying rapid growth of cities, such homes have more and more tended to be in the suburbs. The higher the income, the more satisfactory the personal environment, often including both the home in the pleasant residential suburb and the apartment in the city, the main place of work. That work, and the source of the income with which the well-to-do could afford the suburban retreat, has been integrally tied in with the development of the industrial business of the nation, and with the services necessary to have it operate smoothly in a free market economy.*

But this same industrial development, functioning in the free market, has caused increasing problems of pollution and congestion. For a long time, the well-to-do were not concerned about these problems; until quite recently, they could make their money in the city and buy their ecology in the country. That possibility is rapidly disappearing. Pollution is increasing both in intensity and geographical area. The suburbs have had to move farther and farther out. This has, in turn, meant longer and longer commuting, greater and greater congestion in transportation, and less and less open space, natural areas, and environmental amenities. The attendant growth has also slowly led to overcrowding of resort facilities, vacation places, seashores, mountain lakes, and desert. The split lifestyle—in which the working day is spent in pollution- and congestion-creating activity in the city, and the evening, week-end, and vacation is spent far removed from pollution and congestion—is no longer feasible except for a very small minority. Having the pleasantest residential environment and the most profitable business environment is becoming more and more like having your cake and eating it, too!

The present conservation movement came to maturity as a result of this dilemma. What had previously been the limited, almost eccentric, hobby of a few blossomed suddenly into a major national force across the country. Its socio-economic characteristics, in terms of crime, social class, and ethnic composition, did not change; what changed was the enlarged socio-economic groups from whom conservation drew its supporters. This increase placed vastly greater importance on what the conservationists were about.

---

* Over the last ten years, the relationship between the development of an industrial economy within a free market system and the creation of pollution has been traced out in innumerable works, of which Barry Commoner's *The Closing Circle* is only one of the best known. This is of course not to say that the similar development in a planned economy will necessarily have any different result, as the Stockholm conference saw; what is needed in both cases is a socially-executed purpose to limit the unwanted by-products of economic development.

Escapism or Reform

Two avenues are open to these groups to avoid the dilemma of environmental deterioration stemming from business prosperity—one escapist, the other reformist. The first is to create, socially, possibilities for escape which could no longer be individually achieved; the second is to create, socially, a mechanism for moderating, at their source, the causes of pollution and congestion. The first treats the symptoms, the second the disease. The first is essentially selfish, limited in benefit, short-term and conservative; the second is of general benefit, long-term, and potentially, but not necessarily, radical in its consequences.

Examples of the first (escapist) tendency within the conservation movement are inevitably controversial, but they suggest the differences in approach. BART, in the San Francisco Bay Area, has been heralded as the way in which mass transit may solve the urban transportation crisis. In fact, it may simply be a way by which those who can afford to move 30 miles away from the city to get away from its problems can nevertheless commute to work easily and painlessly, eliminating the need to tackle the tougher problem of living nearer to the city. Limiting growth is a fashionable answer to deterioration of the residential environment: it may offer a fine solution to those who have already made it to the upper-class communities of Long Island, the one-class "new towns" of California, or the suburban enclaves of middle America; but it leaves the problems of the majority of the cities' residents unsolved. Protecting wilderness is a genuine need, and overuse is incompatible with the true "wilderness experience"; but putting a fence around natural areas which are potential recreational resources for millions of people and making them available just for a few is certainly helping the few at the expense of the many. By themselves, these are all essentially escapist approaches to conservation.

On the other hand, the second (reform) tendency within the conservation movement has pressed the assumption of public responsibility for the quality of the environment. This not only means preservation of remote mountain areas and wild rivers, but also reduction of air pollution in the inner cities and water pollution at the public beaches. It means limiting construction in coastal zones, but also opening coastal beaches to public access and use. It means preservation of open space and natural areas not only for migrating waterfowl and rare plants, but also for inner-city children and senior citizens. It means placing certain values on a scale above the profit motive, and a willingness to limit individual rights for the public good. It means questioning the consumer mentality and the desire for unlimited economic growth, and raising questions of equity and ethics as immediate questions for public attention.

In short, then, the rapid growth of the conservation movement over the last 10 years is the direct product of these developments. The operation of the private market and uncontrolled free enterprise has made it harder and harder for even the rich to escape the consequences of pollution, uncontrolled growth, and unrestricted production geared solely to maximizing profit. Upper-class whites have thus found it necessary to ask for government assistance to avoid the unpleasant externalities of the very system from which they themselves have already benefited so extensively.

Both the escapist and the reformist tendencies in the conservation movement have fostered this emphasis on governmental action. This means a direct entry into the political arena; and here the direct confrontation with the inner-city movement arises. For this is the same arena in which inner-city groups have long sought assistance in achieving their own ends. This is why contact between these two groups on environmental issues, never a subject of much interest before, has now become of major concern. The somewhat skeptical reaction evidenced by many inner-city residents and groups, when confronted with this new profession of concern for the

---

"Upper-class whites have . . . found it necessary to ask for government assistance to avoid the unpleasant externalities of the very system from which they themselves have already benefited so extensively."

---

environment in the name of the general public good by upper- and middle-class white establishment types, is perhaps understandable, no matter how well motivated that concern in fact is.* As clash after clash has developed, that skepticism has only increased.

What kind of policies, or approaches, or theories, or alliances, might be developed to handle constructively these clashes that we have already seen to be taking place and that, from this analysis, seem inevitable? How should the conservation movement, or at least those within it concerned with reform rather than escape, respond to the skepticism of the inner-city movement?

The conservation movement's response thus far has been superficial and inadequate. One response is to deny that conflicts exist, and to argue that apparent cases of conflict are rare exceptions. The preponderance of the evidence is to the contrary.

---

* Dr. Faramelli quotes a Chicago community organizer as saying, "What I look forward to least in life is living in a pollution-free, repressive, unjust society."

The other response is to whisk the problem away by moving to a high enough level of generality:

> Both movements should share a commitment to the wholeness of life and should revere it. We should care what happens to all life forms, human and non-human, and work together to secure and maintain sound life-support systems. We have to care about all parts of the human race, and understand that other forms of life have claims upon our conscience, too. A communion of purpose should join us which will cause us to shrink from thinking in terms of trade-offs between life forms and dropping one concern for another.*

Neither response is calculated to earn the respect or confidence of inner-city residents. They lead to what might be called a "first-things-first-second-things-much-later-if-ever" policy. They say to the inner-city resident, "Look, we are all fellow-travelers on spaceship earth; if it doesn't survive, neither will any of us. Therefore we must put ecological concerns first, and forget our petty differences in our common effort to preserve the human race. We have full sympathy for your complaints about being hungry, having wretched housing, being without a job, and so forth, but you must remember that neither food, housing, nor jobs will matter if the whole earth dies." The order of priorities is fixed by environmental, not inner-city, concerns; meeting inner-city needs is a fortunate by-product of an occasional environmentally-motivated action.

Unfortunately, this policy will not do. There *is* a clash of priorities. No appeals to "the wholeness of life" and no number of little bridges to the inner-city movement built to conservationist specifications will change the fact. The examples cited in this paper can be expanded at length; on a larger scale, the 1972 United Nations Conference on the Human Environment in Stockholm saw the same conflict of priorities reveal itself in the differences between developing and developed countries.[24]

Potentials for Change

The bleak picture that emerges from the present analysis is of two groups, one conservationist, the other inner-city, with two different constituencies, with different and often conflicting interests, different goals, and different priorities. I think that picture is essentially correct. But I do not think it follows that this is the way it should be, or that nothing can be done to change it. Change may be possible, and on three levels. For convenience, they might be called the levels of bridge-building, of log-rolling, and of social change. What they have in common is a rejection of the escapist tendency of the conservation movement in favor of its reformist tendency, an honest recognition of differences of priorities, and

---

* Michael McCloskey, editorial, *The Sierra Club Bulletin.*

a willingness to modify the conservationists' own agendas to meet inner-city concerns.

"Bridge-building," fixing on those particular areas where conservation and inner-city interests coincide, has already been criticized as an incom-

---

" 'Log-rolling' is a not-so-nice name for an old and honorable activity in a democracy. . . . It is obvious that conservationists and inner-city residents should work together where bridges exist, where both immediately gain from the specific project; why should they not also work together where only one gains, if the other is not hurt?"

---

plete basis for a constructive relationship. This does not mean that it can be ignored, or that it is not helpful. There are, in fact, a number of areas in which the immediate and direct interests of inner-city and conservationist groups do coincide. Opposition to freeway construction is the example that has probably brought the two groups together most visibly thus far, but there are others: opposition to the noise created by inner-city-located airports, traffic congestion, air pollution; greater open space and recreational facilities; environmental education in the schools; and outdoor summer camps for children. Many of these have in them also ingredients of conflict: open space often is at the expense of housing, pollution-creating industries also create jobs, environmental education is no substitute for sound all-around educational programming. Yet many opportunities for joint action exist.

The conservation movement can do much to maximize these opportunities; it need not sit around waiting for them to happen. The least that can be done is simply to increase contact between the two groups. Conferences such as the one that resulted in the present volume are examples on the national level, but similar opportunities exist locally: recruiting of members can be geared to produce specific contacts, boards can be expanded, friendships can be established, all of which will make conservation groups much more sensitive to the opportunities for mutually desirable action, action that in fact serves the interests of both groups.

"Log-rolling" is a not-so-nice name for an old and honorable activity in a democracy: the trading of votes, or support, by two groups with each other, in areas where both are *not* interested. It is obvious that conservationists and inner-city residents should work together where bridges exist, where both immediately gain from the specific project; why should they not also work together where only one gains, if the other is not hurt? Each needs the other's support; they already have some things in common; and certain philosophic ties bind them together. Such log-rolling has already taken place to some extent; groups such as Environmental Action are in fact specifically devoted to activities that might be thus described, in addition to more conventional bridge-building. But the extent of it is as yet very limited, and Environmental Action and like groups are still among the weakest and youngest of the brethren. Much more can be done. Political leaders on a national and local level (witness Tom Bradley's successful campaign for Mayor in Los Angeles) are probably already more aware of the possibilities here than are the movement's leaders themselves.

Putting its own house in order can also be viewed as a form of log-rolling by the conservation movement. Looking specifically for black park rangers is obviously appropriate in parks or historic sites dealing specifically with black history or culture, as is the hiring of Indians on Navaho sites. To integrate the Park Service from top to bottom might well be a direct object of conservationist pressure. So might development of programs and resources to appeal specifically to the differing backgrounds and interests of inner-city residents, making certain that facilities are specifically available to them, as well as to all others, in terms of location, transportation, and information; and providing subsidies to permit the attendance at meetings and conferences of those financially unable to attend with their own resources. These are all ways that conservationists might go out of their own way to serve the interests of unity between their cause and that of inner-city residents.

In the same way, they should be sensitive to the effects on inner-city residents of their own proposals, many of which need only slight modification to remove quite objectionable and regressive features. The handling of limitations on use of the national parks is a good example: a reservation system by and large affects the poor adversely, since their ability to plan ahead is more limited than that of the middle class. Saving a significant amount of space to be used on a first-come first-served basis is at least one compromise that might better promote unity of the two groups.

"Social change" is a broad phrase that can cover a variety of sins as well as of blessings. The structure of society and the operation of its economic system bear an intimate relationship to concerns of both the inner-city and conservation movements. Many inner-city leaders are convinced that basic changes are needed before social justice and equality can be achieved: changes in the distribution of income, in access to opportunities, in the control of basic institutions, in the structure of government and the political processes. In particular, they feel that the untrammeled operation of the private market, powered by the profit motive, and guiding rather than being guided by the democratically-arrived-at decisions of

30

government, is unlikely to alleviate any of the more significant problems from which the inner-city suffers.

Upper income groups have, until fairly recently, been rather well served by these same structures and market arrangements. That is, after all, how they got where they are. But, as was pointed out above, the unpleasant externalities of the system are beginning to be a serious problem to them, too: pollution, congestion, crime, and ugliness are becoming more and more inescapable. The rich, as well as the poor, need some serious changes in the way things now work. The reform thrust of the conservation movement stems from this realization.

The changes the two groups want appear at first to go in opposite directions. Take the simplest example, redistribution of income, a change most inner-city leaders see as indispensable: this means, after all, *from* the rich *to* the poor, and the rich can hardly be expected to be overjoyed at the prospect. The rich, on the other hand, tend to see the answer to environmental degradation in terms of limiting growth, thus limiting the poor's traditional method of improving their absolute standard of living. One might thus suspect that there would be basic political differences between the two groups, and that the type of social change each wants goes in opposite directions to what the other would want.

Yet, in the long run, both groups have a major interest in social change in a like direction. A Rand Corporation report,[25] studying the ecological effects of various growth strategies on the booming city of San Jose, California, phrases the issue in unusually frank and direct terms:

> The real difficulty, of course, lies not with technology, but with goals and institutions. Increasing productivity is needed because increasing production is needed—needed for the individual goal of being materially better off year after year; needed for the social/political goal of improving the lot of those at the lower end of the income distribution without substantially hurting those at the upper end. And full employment is needed because employment is the only "dignified" way for individuals to gain income.

> It takes a set of Utopian suppositions to move to the "spaceman" economy in which, if economics and ecology cannot be reconciled, at least their conflict can be minimized. Suppose that

> —individuals were to value less highly annual material improvement, so that increases in productivity could be translated into more leisure instead of more production;

> —*re*distribution of income from the better-off to the worse-off became more feasible, so that the poor could be helped without special increments of new production;

> —with living standards supported by a system of social insurance and income guarantees, full employment became no longer a superordinate goal for a healthy economy.

31

Were these to come to pass (and their Utopianism can be measured by the fact that there is no way to discuss the path from here to there except by using the Biblical phrase "come to pass"), then the *overemployment* of resources, environment, and space that goes hand-in-hand with full employment of labor might be drastically reduced.

. . . All this, of course, is a construct . . . Because neither institutions nor technology in San Jose can adapt by themselves, it seems possible that the resolution of the dilemma will lie in part (and involuntarily) in less than full employment, in less than maximum individual material improvement, and in less attention than should be paid to the social problems at the bottom of the income scale . . .

The national solution will have to be one that moves toward the Utopian assumption listed above.[26]

Rand is exactly right; in the long run, it takes a commitment to such "Utopian" goals of social change to accomplish both the ends of the environmentalists and of inner-city residents, and each has much to gain by joining forces with the other in their pursuit.[*]

Such a development would have a real philosophic, as well as practical basis.[27] For, in the long run, the driving spirit behind one part of the conservationist movement is a humane one; one which suggests that certain

---

"If the answer to congestion is to limit further growth, conflicts will be inevitable; if the approach is to provide for such growth positively and effectively, by a social assumption of the responsibility for dealing with its consequences, conflicts will be few."

---

individual and social values, rather than the profit motive, should be the driving force behind the organization of society and the exploitation of its resources. A different attitude towards the natural environment is linked to a different attitude toward the social environment, which after all creates the natural environmental problems with which conservationists are concerned. Exploitation of natural resources will not cease till exploitation of human beings ends. Pushed deeply enough, the goals of conservationists and those concerned with inner-city problems meet. Both are essentially

---

[*] The Report interestingly goes on to suggest that "Santa Clara County does have one safety valve not available to the nation, however—migration . . . parts of San Jose's population would quickly respond to a slow-down of economic growth by migrating out . . . ." In other words, San Jose can limit growth by letting things get so bad that the poor will move out, presumably bringing their problems into someone else's backyard but leaving Santa Clara County a better place for the better-off to live!

32

concerned with eliminating fundamental evils caused by a social structure predicated on maximizing the opportunity for private profit, and both must willy-nilly bend their efforts to changing fundamental features of that society if they are to achieve their ends.

Yet the long-run interests of the two are basically different if the conservation movement is dominated by its escapist tendency, if it seeks to escape the problems created by the system, rather than to solve them. If the answer to vandalism in the parks is the arming of park rangers, the hiring of security guards, and the exclusion and expulsion of visitors thought to be "undesirable," then no common interests will appear; but if it is in the area of meeting the legitimate needs of all potential users, including those who are poor, discriminated against, and exploited, quite a different set of possibilities emerges. If the answer to overuse of the parks is to ration admission by requiring reservations, little can be achieved together; but if the answer is a shift of national priorities to provide substantially greater opportunities for recreation for all segments of society, much can be done. If the answer to congestion is to limit further growth, conflicts will be inevitable; if the approach is to provide for such growth positively and effectively, by a social assumption of the responsibility for dealing with its consequences, conflicts will be few. It is true that the short-run interests of the conservation and inner-city movements often conflict, but it is equally true that the short- and long-run interests of the conservation movement often conflict with each other in precisely the same manner. Were the movement to take a longer perspective on its own needs—not the one billion years of spaceship-earth type thinking, but the one- or two-generation perspective with which most people are really personally concerned when they think deeply about the future—many of its programmatic goals might more closely approximate those of inner-city residents.

There is a real danger in relying on such broad philosophic agreement, however, as a basis for guiding day-to-day actions. In a sense *all* conflicts, whether between nations, individuals, ethnic groups, or social classes, can be resolved only if the level of analysis is raised high enough—if we go "up one system level" or more, and certainly if we go up to the level of the universe, as Wes Churchman not so facetiously suggests. But that is not a very useful approach to solving day-to-day problems, or deciding on political strategy or tactics. It obscures, and thus makes more difficult to handle, the real conflicts that do exist.

Even if conservation goals and inner-city goals are identical at some high level of generality, the means to those goals may be quite different for each group, and one or the other might be hurt much more or less by that choice of means. Both ghetto resident and suburbanite will be better off if use of Yosemite is limited now so it will still be there 50 years from now, but who is kept out now may make a great deal of difference to both.

33

A Crucial Turning Point

The conservation movement is now, I think, at a crossroads. It has been forced into the political arena, and it has acquired substantial strength and experience there. Its escapist tendency has frequently put it into direct conflict with those whose first concerns derive from the inner city; at the same time, its reformist tendency and philosophic commitments have tended to make it sympathetic to inner-city concerns. Thus far, it has tended to ignore the contradictions, sometimes building little bridges in practice, more frequently drowning fuller discussion with flowing generalities. But the political problems are increasing, and the conservation movement may soon have to choose among potential bedfellows. Environmental quality in the suburbs can co-exist for a time with either tighter ghettos in the inner city or with social justice for all, but not with both for long.

The conservation movement already has many interests in common with the inner-city residents, the poor, and minorities, but it by no means has an identity of interests with them. Its own constituency is generally at the opposite end of the social and economic spectrum. If the conservation movement is to be true to the deeper long-range implications of its own concerns, rather than being confined within its class and social origins —if it is to pursue its social reform, rather than its escapist direction—it must make two changes in its present policies. It must begin frankly and honestly to recognize the real differences between it and the inner-city movement, in terms of character as well as short-terms goals, immediate program as well as priorities. Given such frank recognition of differences, it must then be willing to bend its own programs, policies, and priorities to take into account inner-city needs and demands. At least three ways of doing this have been suggested here: bridge-building, log-rolling, and agreement on an agenda of social change. A common solution to the problems of the physical and of the social environment is possible; whether the conservation movement will concern itself with the search for that common solution remains to be seen.

NOTES TO CHAPTER TWO

1. *CF Letter*, the Conservation Foundation, October, 1972, p. 11.
2. The *BART Impact Study* of the Institute for Urban and Regional Development at the University of California at Berkeley, and the research of the Metropolitan Transportation Commission, are beginnings at the effort to deal with these questions explicitly and methodically.
3. Sam Love, "Ecology and Social Justice: Is There a Conflict?", *Environmental Action*, August 5, 1972, p. 5, quoting from the *1971 Annual Report* of the Council on Environmental Quality. Love goes on to say, "'Borne disproportionately' is an economic euphemism for giving someone else the shaft."

A detailed proposal for such a requirement was put forth in a speech by the author before the Suburban Action Institute Conference on "The Environment of the Open Society," New York, N.Y., January, 1973.

5. Carter B. Horsely, "Ecological Zoning Code Sought in Huntington Township," *New York Times*, January 25, 1971, quoted in Richard F. Babcock and David L. Callies, "Ecology and Housing: Virtues in Conflict," Resources for the Future, mimeo., April 14, 1972.

6. Fred P. Bosselman, "Ecology vs. Equality: The Sierra Club Meets the NAACP," *Law and Social Problems*, vol. 2 (Fall 1971), p. 98ff.

7. Sierra Club, *et al.*, vs. George Romney, *et al.*, U.S. District Court, Western District, Texas, 1972, cited in Babcock and Callies, *supra*, p. 8.

8. Fred Bosselman and David L. Callies, *The Quiet Revolution in Land Use Control*, Washington: Government Printing Office, 1971.

9. The Conservation Foundation, *National Parks for the Future*, Washington, D. C. 1972.

10. Norman J. Faramelli, "Economic Growth, Social Justice, and Ecology," Paper Presented at Conference of the Council on Population and the Environment, Northern Illinois University, De Kalb, Ill., May 5, 1972.

11. "The Pending Land-Use Proposals: Will They Meet or Defeat Social Goals?" Paper presented at Conference sponsored by Citizens' Committee on Population and the American Future, Washington, D. C., April 16, 1973, mimeo.

12. At the same time, however, there are some hopeful trends in the conservation movement. It would be presumptuous to try to list the conservationists and conservation groups whose active commitment to social justice is strong, but the works of the Conservation Foundation, Environmental Action, and California Tomorrow; certain actions of the Sierra Club; support by conservation groups of the Suburban Action Institute's proposed development in Mahwah, N. J.; and the formation of the Urban Environment Conference all indicate that the picture painted here is far from all-inclusive.

13. Sam Love, *op. cit.*, p. 5.

14. One of the few, but very limited in scope, is Joseph Harry, *et al.*, "Conservation: An Upper Middle Class Social Movement," *Journal of Leisure Research*, vol. 1 (Summer 1969), pg. 246, and discussion in "A Comment: Conservation: An Upper-Middle Class Social Movement," *Journal of Leisure Research*, vol. 3, (Spring 1971), no. 2.

15. U.S. Department of the Interior, Bureau of Outdoor Recreation, Washington, D. C., 1965, p. 27.

16. Outdoor Recreation Resources Review Commission, Study Report 19, Washington, D. C., 1962, p. 35.

17. Outdoor Recreation Resources Review Commission, Participation in Outdoor Activities: Factors Affecting Demand Among American Adults, Study Report 20, Washington, D. C. 1962, p. 60.

18. U.S. Department of the Interior, Bureau of Outdoor Recreation, *The 1970 Survey of Outdoor Recreation Activities, Preliminary Report*, Washington, D. C., February 1972, p. 58.

19. *Ibid.*, p. 59.

20. *Ibid.*, p. 83.

21. *Ibid.*, pp. 99-101.

22. U.S. Department of the Interior, National Park Service, Washington, D. C., Memorandum N26-N (January 22, 1969), in Doris Y. Wilkinson, "The Class Imperative," *National Parks for the Future, supra*, pp. 241-2.

23. Harry, *supra*; Devall, "Conservation: An Upper-Middle Class Social Movement: A Replication," *Journal of Leisure Research*, vol. 2 (Spring 1970), p. 123; Hendee, *et al.*, *Wilderness Users In the Pacific Northwest: Their Characteristics, Values and Management Preferences*," USDA Forest Service Research Paper PNW-61 (1968).

24. See Barry Commoner, "Motherhood in Stockholm," *Harper's Magazine*, June, 1972, p. 49.

25. Rand Urban Policy Analysis Group, *Alternative Growth Strategies for San Jose*: Initial Report of the Rand Urban Policy Analysis Project. WN-7657-NSF, October, 1971.

26. *Ibid.*, pp. 74-76.

27. For an excellent discussion, see the report on the symposium on "Ecology and Revolution," published in *Le Nouvel Observateur*, no. 397, and reprinted in part in *Liberation*, vol. 17, No. 6 (September, 1972). See also William Leiss, *The Domination of Nature*, and Herbert Marcuse, *Counter-Revolution and Revolt* (Boston: Beacon Press, 1972), ch. 2.

CHAPTER III

Dialogue:
Attitudes Toward
Environmentalism

I. The Inner City—*Senator Richard H. Newhouse*
Illinois State Senate

II. Conservation Groups—*Ted Pankowski, Jr.*
Izaak Walton League of America

III. Organized Labor—*John Yolton*
United Auto Workers

(The following is a condensation of the first session of the Conservation Foundation's conference on environmental quality and social justice. The opening speaker is Illinois State Senator Richard Newhouse, of Chicago.)

I. The Inner City

Senator Newhouse: The urban social movement has been concerned with housing, welfare, unemployment, and youth problems. Insofar as the people in those activities are concerned, there is absolutely no connection between what they see as an environmental movement and what their problems are all about.

The reason that the problems are so basic on this level is that when we speak about environment we speak about scomething a little bit different. Let me give you an idea, from my own district, about what I have reference to. My district in Chicago is a very unique one, sort of a microcosm of the city in that it has some of the poorest amenities and some of the best amenities. It has some very poor people and some very well-to-do people. It has some of the worst educational institutions in the city and one of the best in the country. So there is that kind of paradoxical situation. It has some of the worst slums in the city of Chicago, some of the best housing in the city of Chicago, and it includes two of the largest parks in the city.

The problems are myriad, though, and the reasons for those, in a sense, are political and they have to do with environment. For example, my district includes Woodlawn, the home of the Blackstone Rangers. The problems of Woodlawn, a community that has been totally destroyed while the political people stood around and watched, are really a case history on the environment as it affects blacks. For example, up near here, in the community of Northbrook, about five years ago I read a story in one of the Sunday supplements that the high school senior class had built a home and they were going to sell that home for $60,000 and plow the $60,000 back into an ongoing vocational program for the benefit of youngsters in that specific school. My thoughts were that, for 20 years, young white children from Northbrook will be able to pass by that house and say, "I built that in my senior year," and then go off to Lakewood and get on their polo ponies.

Meanwhile, my kids—back at 64th and Bedford, where the community is falling in around their heads—cannot get the opportunity to drive a nail for very political reasons. Some of the political reasons relate to the building and construction trades unions which will not permit a vocational training program to exist in an area where it certainly ought to be the first priority.

Young men grow up in that community from families whose backgrounds are probably pretty much the same. The first generation came up from the rural South, and they are either the second or third generation, having never seen any open space except when they stumble into the parks —parks that they are afraid to use. So talking about open space is not likely to draw a great deal of attention in the pool room.

You asked about the fact that the normal outlet for their growth has been shut off. Let me describe this for you very briefly because, it seems to me, you have to understand the basis for this. In the politically organized white communities in the city of Chicago, for example—I'm talking about the blue-collar working districts now—a baby is born and the doctor slaps the baby on the behind, and the baby cries, and the momma laughs and the poppa laughs. Over in my district, they slap the baby on the behind, and the baby cries, and the momma cries, and wherever the daddy is, he cries, too.

Now their problem is: what are they going to do with this little thing? Who has the wherewithal to support it, to buy it food? You lose 20 per cent of your children there. Then, after that, you talk about what is required to get clothing and get it in school, and you lose another 20 per cent. And then you talk about what is required to provide it with safety, both from thugs in the street and danger in the street and the police department, and you lose another 10 or 20 per cent of these kids. By the time you get to high school, you've lost 70 per cent of your children.

Well, between high school and drop-outs, it's pretty hard to tell what does happen. Contrast that with the white, politically organized community

38

where you slap the baby, and the momma laughs and the daddy laughs because it's known what life plan has been made out for that child. If he's absolutely stupid and lazy, he learns to work in the building construction trades at $5 an hour. If he has a nickel's worth of sense and can finish high school, there's a spot reserved for him, either on the police department or the fire department, where he can start working at $12,000 per year on a job in which he can either moonlight in one direction or continue his education in the other. If he decides to continue his education, he goes to night law school, and from there to the state's attorney's office, where he practices law at the public's expense. If he has a half a spark after that, he goes on the bench and becomes a judge. And, so, a large percentage of the judges in the city of Chicago take precisely this route.

Now, what connection does this have? Well, first of all, there isn't any money to talk about conservation or anything else. There's a scramble for existence that simply causes deterioration in every other segment of life. So, when you talk about the quality of life, what you're talking about is what kind of extralegal or illegal activity can I participate in that will permit me to survive. Now, don't you admit that it's kind of silly to talk about conservation of resources? Because there aren't any resources. All life's energies are taken up with just plain existence. Now, that's the first thing you've got to deal with.

The conservation movement is much the same as women's lib and all the rest of the elitist operations that have come into being since people got sick and tired of fighting for the rights of black people. It's certainly seen as a siphoning off of all the energies of some good people who previously dedicated themselves to an end that people could see as a desirable one.

Now, if you look at this from a politician's viewpoint—and I am—you've got some very selfish interests to be served by frustrating the program that I see must be constructed in order for there to be any participation on the part of the minority community in the subject that you have in mind. Let me go back to my own community.

I mentioned to you that Woodlawn is in the center of my district and that the other communities on the edge of that are deteriorating in like manner. South Shore, which used to be a very desirable community, is now feeling the effect of the movement pressures from Woodlawn, where it's been completely destroyed and families had to go somewhere. Oakland has been destroyed, and so pressures are put upon Hyde Park. Now, we have two parks in this district, and one of the things we have done in our political dealings is to pull together a recreation committee. Now this recreation committee wasn't pulled together with any high-minded thoughts about environmental quality. We were trying to figure out how to save our kids. The theory was that they spend a good deal of their lives in the classroom, and if there wasn't some kind of empathetic kind of atmosphere for them to proceed to when they came outside the classroom, the chances of their gaining anything from classroom experience or anywhere else were pretty well watered down.

Secondly, we saw, through a recreation committee, an opportunity to begin to permit young people to see some things that they hadn't previously seen. It's no secret that youngsters were born in Woodlawn, grew up in Woodlawn, and died in Woodlawn without getting very far beyond its boundaries.

"The politics of urban society, it seems to me, pretty much mitigate against everything we're talking about, for the reason that urban society . . . depends upon having something in the nature of a scapegoat that must be deprived in order that there be more to split up among those who share in the proceeds of the political pie."

One of the things that we attempted to do was to provide some kind of correlation between the people who ran the park system and the people in the community. It seemed to us that if the park system had any relevance at all, it ought to be planning ways to make it pleasant for people to use parks. The two parks were never used. One of the parks had an Olympic-sized children's swimming pool—it's really a marvelous facility that hasn't been used in four years. One reason is that people were afraid. The second is that the bathhouse was permitted to become a slum. They simply wouldn't paint it. Simple things like this.

So the problem becomes—how does a politically weak and disorganized community get the park board, which is presided over by a young man who wants to be mayor of the city, to paint a bathhouse? You have to reduce it to those kinds of terms. And there were some other concerns, too. They had a lagoon over there that was just a filthy mess. It was a simple matter of getting the lagoon cleaned and providing some kind of water movement which would have made it a much more pleasant place for people to come and spend some quiet time.

The politics of urban society, it seems to me, pretty much mitigate against everything we're talking about for the reason that urban society—and the politics of it, as I see it from a Chicago perspective—depends upon having something in the nature of a scapegoat that must be deprived in order that there be more to be split up among those who share in the proceeds of the political pie. Let me just explain to you very quickly what I mean by that.

There was some movement in Chicago to require policemen to live in the city. There was a big fight going on about that. What are they really talking about? They're talking about something very simple. They're not going to recruit any blacks or minorities on the police force in spite of the fact that the community will soon be black and minorities. What they're going to do is keep blacks and minorities off the force because these are well-paid patronage jobs which have a great deal of political clout.

It is artificially preserving a political system that ought to change anyway. The political system is almost the natural enemy to everything we're trying to do, if you want to look at it from the perspective of what we do about our metropolitan areas and what we do about our state.

A good deal of this is rambling, but I guess you want me to reflect on what I feel are the deepest things we have to reach for in order to get some kind of cooperation between these two elements. I say—very, very clearly—that it's going to be an extremely difficult job. So where is hope? Is there any? I think that, possibly, there is.

It seems to me that in any movement that proceeds there is a very definite need to tie in with those who most need to be protected. Some groups will have to be reached on the level of providing some sophistication to the handling of their own political problems. For example, let me talk a moment about the welfare movement as I see what's happening from a state-house level. I know of the existence of the Welfare Rights Organization and two or three other groups, but at no time have any of those organizations ever approached me as a member of the Welfare Committee. I feel very sad about that. As a member of the Appropriations Committee, they have never approached me, as an organization, to talk about what kind of lobbying tactics they ought to be doing.

I sit on the Welfare Committee, for example, and people who think they're doing good bring down to Springfield a group of welfare mothers, all of whom are obese. The diet is such that that's what's going to happen to them. The effect upon those downstate legislators, who hate welfare in the first place and hate welfare mothers even more heartily than they hate welfare, their reaction is that here's this big fat chick, overweight and overfed—let's cut the budget. Now, with a little forethought, you could find certain welfare mothers—skinny and who lost sons in Vietnam—and bring them down, with their Gold Stars on, to face the National Rifle Association.

One of the things I can see that can come out of this sharing of ideas is an interchange of what I see as the shortcomings of some "do-good" organizations which ought to know better and, at the same time, absorb from these same kinds of organizations some sophistication as to what they're trying to do and how the two pieces can be brought together. If anything I've said can help to promote those two ends, I think it was worthwhile.

DISCUSSION

Ann Roosevelt (Friends of the Earth): You said, I think, that the environmental movement was siphoning off people who should be working in civil rights or something like that. Assuming that none of us are going to quit the environmental movement, what are the areas in which we can help? For instance, lead-paint poisoning and lead in the air are consumer issues, but I think we have to get involved in that kind of thing.

Newhouse: Well, that's a beginning. Let's talk about the issue of equality of employment and be very specific. At some point, someone is going to have to take over the building construction trades union. If, within the city of Chicago, tomorrow morning every kid over 17 was put to work with a hammer and a nail, you couldn't build the city fast enough. But artificially induced labor shortages not only cause the costs to go out of sight, but simply destroy the city.

Nobody has taken these guys on. Nobody has really talked to them about the kinds of destruction they are causing. They have become part of the political machine. Somehow, the covers have to be pulled off the Hubert Humphreys and all the rest of these guys who are permitting labor to do the kinds of things it's doing under the guise of having the interest of the small person at heart. I don't know how you do it, but it's got to be done.

This is basic, it seems to me. If young men, energetic and with some feeling for life, can't find some constructive outlet for their energies—that is to say, satisfactory kinds of jobs where they can do things that they see are constructive, if they are not enabled to either marry or, under the new life style, live with the girl they get pregnant and support her (which results in reducing the welfare rolls)—all these things have some specific kind of correlation. I think people understand what the correlation is. If you say that the environment is important, which includes housing and all the rest of it, then how do we work on it?

John Hampton (National Tenants Organization): Let me just say that, in working in Washington with the Urban Environment Conference, the thing I sometimes saw was a feeling that "we're going to come save you"—an attempt by the environmental movement to bring some light or shed some hope on the urban movement, which doesn't work anyway. It strikes me that the opportunity is now here to talk about those two movements—the urban movement, representing the inner-city minority, and the environmental movement, representing a great section of the white population in the suburbs who have some concern about what will happen in the city. The possibility is now here, I think, for those two movements to get together for sheer survival. Survival offers the possibility that maybe

42

we can get together on broader kinds of things than would have been possible under the "let's-get-together-for-good-will-purposes" kind of coalition.

II. Conservation Groups

Ted Pankowski, Jr. (Environmental Affairs Director, Izaak Walton League of America): During the riots in Washington several years ago, reporter Duff Thomas stood in front of the White House and watched the town burn. His comments struck me as being particularly significant, and I would like to share them with you. He said:

> There is now an American understanding gap of outstanding proportions. Cities are man-made monsters and Negroes are striking at those monsters with everything they have. Programs that have barely been inaugurated do little more than nibble, like the rat that runs free in a child's bed. The evils of the American status quo are repugnant beyond description and the very survival of personal freedom is at stake, and unless Americans get on with great speed to change the thinking, the moralities and the very landscape of its sins, it will go the way of all empires. It will take unthinkable ideas put into practice to change contemptible reality that screams at us for change.

For the most part, I believe that the environmental answer to Thomas's remarks has been a collective "ho-hum." Those in the environmental community who do understand that cities have to be our bag, too, are terribly frustrated. They don't know how or where to begin.

"Like most Americans, conservationists don't seem to love our cities. What you don't love, you don't spend money on."

There's kind of a cliché in our business that the hope of conservation is in the cities. Here are the people, the resources, the financing, the talent, the political support. But the thing to be saved is actually still out there in the 19th century West, in the Jeffersonian dream where every man has 20 acres and a mule. Environmentalists started out *there* with conservation, and it seems risky business to throw their money and manpower into the complicated seductions of the wicked and very dangerous city.

Like most Americans, conservationists don't seem to love our cities. What you don't love, you don't spend your money on. And if, indeed, the conservationist is someone who can be unhappy anywhere, as he's been termed, then better he should be unhappy out *there* than in *here,* where most people live.

And so there are significant public attitudes that conservationists are going to have to change within their own constituencies. I think that

---

> *"The fact is that the environmental community has yet to determine its own priorities within its traditional bag, much less branch out into new areas of endeavor."*

---

organized conservation, at least from the top down, is making a good, but faltering effort to change them.

There is the more subtle problem, though, of environmental involvement in urban America. In a 1971 *Washington Evening Star* column, Sterling Tucker wrote:

> Focussing upon the broad areas of water pollution, air pollution and conservation, ecologists are working toward the development of long-range plans which will make tomorrow's America a bit more palatable. Black environmental interests, on the other hand (and, for the suburban birth-watcher who puts up most of the dollars for conservation, black and urban are thought of as being one and the same thing), center on those ecological problems which threaten the present day-to-day existence, on the immediate problems of everyday survival in an increasingly hostile environment.

The key words in Mr. Tucker's article are not "black," "white," "urban," "suburban," but "tomorrow," "long-range," "day-to-day," and "everyday survival." As Senator Newhouse has suggested, it seems to me that the problems that we have to face are not only political, but economical.

Moreover, Sterling Tucker was almost right, for the fact is that the environmental comunity has yet to determine its own priorities within its traditional bag, much less branch out into new areas of endeavor. Until recently, we have not been planning for the future, but reacting to change on an issue-by-issue basis. Environmental leaders who understand, and they are damned few, that the survival needs of the present and of the future are inextricably linked have a tough time convincing their own constituency to divert overcommitted resources from the brush-fires toward urban and very persistent concerns.

As a result, we have under discussion for tomorrow's panel a topic, "Controlling Growth," rather than a topic on the power of positive development and meeting both social and environmental needs.

44

Finally, those environmental groups that have made good-faith efforts to identify and assist in urban affairs desperately need some kind of hand-holds that come from the urban community itself, as well as an agenda that is translatable to people who are defending woods, water, and wildlife, and who exercise their own brand of paternalism with respect to our budget and our priorities.

In my judgment, we—as people who are concerned about both the city and the environment—can use an interface, some kind of a process or mechanism, built on the work that's been begun by the Urban Environment Conference, professionally organized, to follow through on some everyday bridge-building on specific issues. It's really great when the interests of Gary, Indiana, and Beverly Shores mesh so well as to create an Indiana Dunes Lakeshore that's a recreational spot for everyone. And in the teeth of the industrial giants, to boot! Or when we join together in stopping a Three Sisters Bridge. Or in providing jobs for city kids through a Youth Conservation Corps. Or in trying to take Bolling Air Force Base from the Pentagon for the purposes of private urban restoration.

But these bridges somehow get burned down in almost blind clashes. The Bureau of Outdoor Recreation, for example, recently proposed use of the federal Land and Water Conservation Fund for development of *indoor* recreation facilities, particularly in the cities. Our environmental community reacted to this proposal with a knee-jerk "No." And this occurred at a time when we should have seriously considered the possibility that a combined effort between the cities and conservationists could bring the Land and Water Conservation Fund up to a level of spending that would serve both our needs.

I'm deeply concerned that this kind of opportunity seems to slip by us on a regular basis for lack of some kind of way of communicating these things. Attempting to work together, it's quite possible that our joint, really significant contribution to the cities and society, as a whole, may not be environmental improvement itself, as much as we think that must come about, but, in Duff Thomas's words, "in helping to change the thinking, the morality, the very landscape of our sins."

I think this is the cause of a lot of urban problems, and it's certainly going to be the cause of a lot of problems that environmentalists are going to have to face in the future if they don't get with it.

DISCUSSION

Peter Borrelli (Sierra Club): Ted [Pankowski] and the Senator [Newhouse] to a certain extent are pleading with us to blend our politics, if not our issues. I think those of us who have tried blending the issues have found that that's sometimes very difficult, since blending the issues very often obscures the political force associated with those issues. Politically, you can't be saving national parks and improving minority housing at the same time. In state legislatures or the halls of Congress, that kind of marriage is too incomprehensible. And, in the very cruel rest of the world, we have to make our political force as specific as possible. The fact of the matter is that we (environmentalists) have developed a constituency over the years that is uniquely well prepared to address itself to some of the environmental issues, but I find it rather inflexible in addressing itself to some of the broad, urban, social issues that we'll probably be talking about. I know that it is absolutely valid with respect to my own organization, which is both a criticism as well as an observation of its inherent strength. I think that, if we are going to address ourselves to some of the things which the Senator has mentioned and the challenge which Ted has laid before us, we have to talk of ways of either changing that constituency or of educating it.

Keith Roberts (attorney, San Francisco): Just to throw out something a bit contrary, let me suggest that environmentalists are not concerned with urban problems and it's really a mistake to ask them to be. I don't think that there are a great many issues of strong mutual interest that are all that important to either the black people in the city or the environmentalists.

"I detect a note of falseness at the call that environmentalists broaden their concerns and, out of charity and liberalism of heart, start including in their agendas programs to help the benighted slums of the city."

People point to instances where blacks or chicanos have made common cause with the environmentalists. They could, if they were so disposed, point to environmentalists who made common cause with U.S. Steel against the blacks, and vice versa. Instances of temporary, fleeting alliances don't mean anything in terms of building great bonds of mutual interest. The environmentalists, in the history of the movement, came from a concern *not* with the *urban* environment, but with *natural* environment—which, as the Senator pointed out, is something that a lot of people living in the city and a lot of blacks haven't yet had a chance to get out to.

So, I don't think that those kinds of things form a realistic basis for mutual concern. I detect a note of falseness at the call that environmentalists broaden their concerns and, out of charity and liberalism of heart, start including in their agendas programs to help the benighted slums of the city. I don't think that's in the environmentalists' interest.

Carl Pope (Zero Population Growth): I think that Keith's point is very real. Narrow-issue coalitions are probably necessary to get people together and talking to each other. But what I'd like to suggest is that the basic community of interests which we share is at a much broader level. The whole issue is the way in which society has treated blacks since at least 1860, and how the environment has fared since at least 1900. A lot of good people down through the years have worked on both issues. I think it's fair to say that the results haven't been very encouraging.

I saw a newspaper article the other day which suggested that, in the last 40 years, distribution of income in this country hasn't changed a bit. That's in 40 years with lots of citizen activism, lots of groups picking a narrow range of issues and trying to go after that narrow range of issues and trying to do something.

At the time that Nixon came out with the new economic policy, some people in Washington tried to get public-interest groups, labor unions, urban groups and environmental groups together to talk about the fact that every one sort of had a perception that their particular set of interests was getting screwed; that this whole set of things was not in their interest. An attempt was made to try to formulate some sort of response to that, at the level of getting all these people together and saying, "Hey, we're all getting screwed by this"—because we were getting screwed, in different ways and on different issues, but by the same set of economic forces.

It didn't work. I can't speak for everybody, but I know that one of the reactions was that these groups—urban groups and environmental groups—weren't used to doing business that way. They weren't used to generalizing from their issues because it made enemies for them which they didn't want to make. It involved taking on people that they didn't have to take on. It interfered with their ability to make the kinds of coalitions that we all make and that we all rely on to do our political business.

And so nobody was willing to define, in a significant way, an interest broader than absolutely necessary. And yet, because we wouldn't do this, we find ourselves unable to make a response to the basic ways in which power and wealth are distributed in our society.

I would just like to suggest that, unless those basic patterns are changed, it is probably true that there is not enough in the pie, once you let the powerful have what they've got, for both the blacks and the environmentalists. Now, I don't know how organizations with the kinds of history and the kinds of structures that our organizations have get out of that bag. But unless we do, I don't think that very much that is fruitful is likely to come out of this.

Lee Botts (Lake Michigan Federation): Dick Newhouse is my Senator, and let me explain something about the Chicago park situation that he didn't. The city of Chicago is letting the parks fall into ruin because the city regards them as open space to be exploited to solve its housing relocation problems. There is a mutual interest in preserving the parks between those blacks who know, as do many whites, that we don't have to use the parks in Chicago to build housing. If the city administration would be willing to use the pieces of space that are scattered throughout Chicago, it would solve the problem.

Some people want to save the parks because the trees are there, but some other people might want to save the parks in order to force the city to scatter the housing throughout the city and do away with segregation. Maybe there are some other issues like that that we could get together on.

The fight to save the Indiana Dunes is another example. The conservationists and Mayor Hatcher and his administration in Gary are both working to save the Dunes, and maybe we should be looking for those areas where we might not have exactly the same goals to start out with but have a mutual interest in accomplishing something.

III. Organized Labor

John Yolton (United Auto Workers, Detroit): I know that my remarks, to be really meaningful, should probably pass on some words of wisdom or gems of spiritual guidance that, in some way, would help you better understand blue-collar attitudes about the environmental movement. It's much easier to talk about their attitudes toward the environment specifically than it is to talk about the movement—because many of them aren't aware of the movement itself. So, obviously, I'll have to spend most of my time on attitudes toward the environment, and not on the movement. However, don't take what I say to really reflect the true UAW blue-collar attitude because I think the old saying is still true—you can't really know one unless you are one.

The point is that you have all kinds of attitudes. When you talk about *suburban* blue-collar, you're talking about something a hell of a lot different than *inner-city* blue-collar and their attitudes. On the one hand, you're talking about people with money, with boats, with cottages. On the other hand, you're talking about some of the poorest, most destitute people that there are—they are blue-collar, too, and work in some of our factories. Their attitudes are a lot different. We had a very trying experience in Chrysler 212, when we went in to do some rabble-rousing and try to get them motivated, because they weren't really doing as much as we wanted on an environmental program.

They took off on us about what in the hell were we doing, worrying about this (environmental issue). This was not rank and file, for the most part, but secondary local leadership—stewards, committeemen who handle grievances. They were more concerned about gas and fumes, heat, dust that kills inside the plant. And we have not fully solved that problem, of course. They're also concerned more about rats and things where they

48

live, and why don't we, as a union environmental department, do something about *those things,* rather than dream up new ideas.

For the most part, we don't reach the rank and file because our structure is so big—we've got 1,600,000 or so working in the plants, with another million retirees. We usually only reach the secondary leadership in the unions. These are the ones you have to go to first because nothing's going to work unless the "trickle-down" theory that we use works. That is, we educate the secondary leadership, we set up committee people in each factory, and give them ways that they can reach the rank and file through whatever media they have—handbills, local newspapers or, better, personal contact inside the plant.

"When you talk about suburban blue-collar, you're talking about something a hell of a lot different than inner-city blue-collar and their attitudes."

We have mixed reactions from them. Some don't feel we should be spending our money this way, or our energies, or having national staff, as we do, working on these problems. They don't see why we should always be bothering them to get telegrams or letters in because some environmental coalition that we're involved in in Washington says that it's important that we get the letters and telegrams in on a piece of legislation. They're not really ready to march, either.

I don't think any of this should be news to you, because I think a lot of you have tried to make contacts with various different labor unions to get support. It's hard to obtain. We have a devil of a time even when our credentials are good inside our own union. We think we have a couple of hundred thousand, at least, within our membership all over the U.S. and Canada who are what you would call conservation-conscious or environmentally conscious people. They will come forward.

It's a good group that we have. However, out of 1.6 million, this is still a small minority of our membership. It's not that they lack sophistication so much. As far as age is concerned, half of our membership is under 30. They average between a semester and a year in college. So they're not completely removed. It's a different bag of members. We still have long-standing sportsmen and conservation supporters who have not yet retired, but there's no real way that we can accurately analyze the rank-and-file members.

What environmental issues do the members rally around? Among the fishermen, it's water-pollution control. In other areas, it's air pollution. Surveys of our membership, done by the University of Michigan in the River Rouge-Wyandotte area—down-river from Detroit—show their chief concern to be air pollution. Terrible problems there. People sick all the time, kids sick all the time, paint coming off.

Well, we went to them where they lived because we couldn't get them to the union hall. We punched out the computer and got their addresses and wrote them a personal letter, based on the air-pollution factor. We had them come to a school or the union hall where they lived to help solve their problems.

After that, we tried to back off and lose our identity and make it a community thing. A lot of professional people don't want to work with the UAW, so we get it started and then back out of the leadership role. They organize and work together better with a doctor or somebody like that as chairman than with a UAW leader.

So there it was air pollution. They could care less about water pollution, even though the Rouge River had previously caught on fire.

And then, you get open space. Sometimes, we get into vest-pocket parks and interest people where they live. But the best success we've had was to go to them where they live and find that one program that they've got a real interest in. Obviously, our guys (at the Fairchild plant) in Hagerstown, Maryland, weren't interested in stopping the SST, even though we were. They came down in buses, rented by the company, saying, "UAW for the SST." Obviously, we wouldn't talk to them about the SST.

You have to personalize each issue. In the Quad Cities, it's the nuclear plant. Around the Great Lakes, we can organize support for the Steelworkers' fight against Reserve Mining and their dumping into Lake Superior. The same thing with Big Cypress, when we were working on the Everglades National Park. It's hard, outside of Florida, to get people all stirred up and write letters and send telegrams, even though it's for a National Park they someday might want to enjoy.

But, basically, the whole thing really comes down to jobs and income. Guys would rather have pollution as part of their job than not have a job at all. Until we have some real type of redistribution of wealth and income, as well as national planning, in this country—we've never had national planning for people—I don't think it makes any difference what the population is. We've never planned for people in this country! I don't necessarily think cutting the population or stabilizing the growth would solve the problem by itself, unless we plan for the people who are there. We don't plan jobs, we don't plan anything.

We have a shortage of jobs that I'm sure will get worse in the next four years, and workers are immediately faced with the fear thing. That's a horrible thing to have—just living week to week and going in debt. Maybe it's the first decent job—not that working in a factory is always a decent job—that you've had in years. Some of the so-called hard-core unemployed who have been hired in the last couple of years are the first ones to be laid off because of lack of seniority.

When they're faced with this, and then a company spokesman or a politician says, "Look, these environmental eco-freaks want this legislation through" or "They want us to build this expensive thing and buy abatement hardware we can't afford," our people react badly, in spite of the education we do. You see whole communities turned around—workers, so-called liberal state representatives, state senators, congressmen. Dow Chemical got 15,000 people in Midland to rally, saying they wanted the nuclear power plant now and to hell with whether it's safe or anything else. At this point, Democratic congressmen and so-called liberal Republicans are all going back to Washington to make sure that the AEC puts that baby through right now. This is a form of environmental blackmail.

More specifically, if a plant cries that it can't afford to buy any of this pollution-abatement stuff, that they're going to shut down and lay some people off if some standard is enforced or if a more stringent standard is passed by Washington or the state legislature, then the whole community starts getting aroused. They turn on us. And, at that point, we have no economic protection for them other than state unemployment compensation, which is no real answer. That's why we've started these national coalitions to try to get legislation passed that will make it against the law to scare people with the loss of their jobs.

We had some success with the Clean Water bill, which just passed. Section 507 of the new law sets up hearings for companies that cry wolf, saying that they can't afford to purchase pollution-abatement equipment. It also contains a partial environmental Bill of Rights for workers, to give them the right to go and complain about what their factory's doing to pollute the environment, without fear of retribution. It gives them some protection in other ways, too. We had some economic protection for workers who are displaced in the Economic Development Bill, which was, of course, vetoed.

So, at this point, we feel that if a law can be passed against using environmental blackmail, then we'll all be better off, including the environmental-conservation groups who get really shafted on some legislation and enforcement because of economic blackmail—job-loss fear.

DISCUSSION

Wayne Redus (San Francisco Human Rights Commission): It is true that oftentimes a factory will relocate to an area that is more lax in pollution-control requirements. It's also true that a factory will, at times, lay off people. But it's also true that factories will threaten to do that. Their first public reaction will be, "Well, it looks like we're going to have to lay off so many people." Union Carbide, in January, 1971, claimed that they would have to lay off 625 workers at its Marietta, Ohio, plant just to comply with EPA standards.

It was a total BS statement, but it sort of rallied the labor guys around them. On the other hand, the president of the Oil, Chemical & Atomic Workers came out with a public statement that they resented the fact that Union Carbide was using the union members as pawns, just to get across the ecology thing. So the idea of relocation and losing a job is a reality, but it's also a whole "mind" job which is being done. A lot of locals are not reacting to it in public statements.

Pankowski: With respect to the fear of job-loss, could we just turn it around a little bit and look at it in another way? We know there's a tremendous environmental need in this country which is going to require a whole range of people with skills and training and just plain manual skills in order to get a clean-up job done. I'm wondering if anybody, and perhaps the labor unions are in a good position to do this, is pulling together and trying to document what environmental improvement could mean in the way of increased jobs. What could it mean in the way of more work opportunities?

Yolton: It depends on what you spend. It's like the Clean Water Bill—I don't know whether we'll ever get the full appropriations. We've got some figures on what it would cost to clean up America, but I wouldn't quote them. Why, it would take every man, woman, and child the next 30 or 40 years, working full-time and maybe around the clock, to do the things that have to be done.

Angela Rooney (National Coalition for the Transportation Crisis): I think one of the things that make blackmail possible in this business of the environment-versus-jobs argument is the complete lack of economic information on what will actually happen. There's almost nothing you can come up with to counter that argument.

There's another thing, too—a very small bridge, but important. For a long time, I labored in the inner-city problems with no contacts at all with the conservation movement and no feedback. Then, all of a sudden, it began to come—in the field of air pollution—and it was a beautiful thing when it happened. It strengthened everyone's position all the way around.

Instead of calling it environment and conservation, let's call it public health once in a while. The word "environment" has all sorts of unfortunate connotations. Almost a defeatist attitude about it. When you're in the inner city or in any real hard crunch with a tough political problem—which all of these things are—it helps if you can relate the problem very flatly and specifically. Bad air and bad water is not what people like to push aside as the environment—it's public health!

Roberts: There was a labor-environmental conference in San Francisco a couple of years ago that had something to do with this. They have

52

been trying to create a staff potentially for a union in the Bay area to look at environmental problems and to look precisely at these kinds of things because one of the great weaknesses has been that, in some cases, the unions don't know their own self-interests and have to believe what the chamber of commerce tells them.

"Unless we can really become involved in the kinds of primary issues and gut issues and concerns that confront people in the inner city, we can forget about it. We don't have a contribution to make. They're not concerned about our interpretation of the environment."

Lawrence Burr (State Park Commission for the City of New York): Let me add a word in relation to this matter of employment with respect to conservation projects. In New York City, which is developing one of the largest pollution projects I know of in the country, I talked to one of the men who was in charge of this phase of the construction. He said he could use three times the number of local residents—people who had come to him, who want to work, are ready to work but who don't have any standing with the craft unions. He said he could take these men and develop training programs and make them productive workers in half the time that it takes dealing through the craft unions. You talk about environment and environmental quality in the inner city, you're talking about an employment picture which you really don't know. I would guess that, in a city like New York, with black employable males, the rate of unemployment might run up to 40 per cent. Nobody has actually attempted to measure the extent of unemployment among black males in New York.

Then, against this rate of unemployment, you get the so-called New York Plan and the Philadelphia Plan, and so on. The so-called New York Plan is supposed to pick up and train 800 young men for union membership, which will guarantee them continued employment at union rates. And out of 800, how many do they have? Less than 200.

It's a farce. Unless we can really become involved in the kinds of primary issues and gut issues and concerns that confront people in the inner city, we can forget about it. We don't have a contribution to make. They're not concerned about our interpretation of the environment.

53

Borrelli: Peter [Marcuse]* raised the question of the difference between politicizing issues and creating the so-called practical, political alliance of divergent interests. I think one of the big mistakes of the McGovern campaign was the belief that if you found all the divergent interests —the chicanos, the women, the blacks, the environmentalists, the disenchanted Republicans—and told them that they were divergent and that they were all being stomped upon by the status quo, then they would all coalesce and there would be a new, practical political alliance. But the fact of the matter is that they don't have much in common.

The only kinds of practical alliances that are going to develop are alliances that, to a certain extent, find those issues in the social arena that can be personalized for the maximum number of people. It's not enough just to tell people that they're disenfranchised and not part of the system, and that their interests are divergent from the status quo.

Furthermore, I think that when we talk about creating this kind of practical political alliance and the trade-offs that you speak of, we are really talking about a level of political sophistication that I don't believe exists within a lot of those divergent interests, I find, on the whole—despite all our talk of political and environmental action—that the average so-called environmentalist is politically naive. They are far less powerful than we would like to give them credit for.

Then, to compare the environmental movement politically with the labor movement is misleading. It's not a movement that has a political power base to begin with. I think we're being too gratuitous in our conversations today, assuming that the political power that the environmentalists have can be divvied up. For the most part, the environmentalists are powerless.

Peter Marcuse (School of Architecture and Urban Planning, UCLA): If it were agreed that an alliance is required, I think I would say: go for social justice and try to educate the environmentalists on what injustice is to them, rather than going for environmental quality and trying to convince the poor what's in it for them.

The other thing I think I would say is that the environmentalists are not at all powerless, in traditional political terms, as you suggest. True, they are not sophisticated politically at the ward level because they have never had to be. They've had it their way. The freeways get built. In the suburbs, they are all-powerful and don't have to go to town meetings because the town manager knows which side his bread is buttered on. The suburbs run that way.

If the environmentalists wanted to make a major part of their program opening up existing suburbs to low-income housing, they would be tremendously powerful because they and their friends are in the driver's seat.

---

* See Marcuse's essay, "Conservation For Whom?," Chapter II of this book.

Hampton: Peter [Marcuse], I hear you saying something far more damning of society and far more complicated. I hear you saying—accepting that the system doesn't work except for a very few—that the system not only abuses natural resources, but abuses human resources.

I think you are correct in that the short-range picture is dismal except in a very few instances. But only in the long range does the true power of both the urban and environmental coalitions become very obvious. In the short range, it doesn't. If everyone accepts what you say, what do we do here if the short range is kind of dismal and the long range is attractive?

Pope: I think we have two kinds of analyses going on, and I think they both can be drawn out here very quickly. On the one hand, we have an analysis from an organizational perspective of where the environmental organizations are and what they think they know how to do and what they think they can do to bring their constituents along. Then again we have an analysis of where are we trying to go and then, working back logically and systematically from where we want to go, of what the necessary steps are to get us there.

I think it's probably evident that the two don't come anywhere near to meeting. Intellectually, that may be a realistic appraisal—that is, there may not be a way out of the bind. But in terms of the question you asked—where do we go—there is a very great danger at a meeting like this, when we are all free from normal organizational constraints, to start trying to draw up an agenda for the nation. That might be a fairly easy thing to do, but, in fact, that is not what we do in our day-to-day work.

I would like to see us focus in on the kind of resources which we here actually control, which are not the hearts and minds of any segment of the American people, but some fairly concrete resources which lie within certain public-interest organizations which have constituencies. I'd like to suggest, for example, that income redistribution is one of the things that needs to be on the common agenda.

Pankowski: Peter [Marcuse], you seem to be laying a lot of the urban sins on the conservation community, as if they caused them. I would like to tell you about proposed land-use legislation. Here is a bill which seeks not to stifle growth necessarily, but redirect it. The impetus for that bill came out of the conservation community, which was concerned about the growth of the suburbs and about the whole question of urban sprawl, strip cities, creating landfills on public coasts and shorelines for any damned thing any developer wanted to put on them. The people who objected to being covered by that legislation weren't conservationists; it was the National League of Cities. They don't want the controls. So don't lay it all on us.

Marcuse: The point Ted [Pankowski] makes is a very important one. The national urban growth policy and implementing legislation—and we're way ahead of the rest of the world in California because we had the

55

problems sooner—is designed around the conception that sees the preservation of land as the prime focus and that defines areas of critical environmental concern. It then suggests that, nationally and on the state level, initial attention be focused on areas of critical environmental concern.

What areas are those? Are those the inner cities? No. What they're talking about in California are the coasts, the desert areas, and the fringes of the major cities. They are talking about the only land left where there is a possibility of constructing new low-income housing. The concern, in at least some cases, is with protecting existing suburbs against low-income and minority neighbors. I think one of the fastest things which the environmental movement could do to forge some kind of political alliance is to make it crystal-clear that it will have nothing to do with racist land-use regulations, and for the Sierra Club, the Izaak Walton League, and the

---

"I think one of the fastest things which the environmental movement could do to forge some kind of political alliance is to make it crystal-clear that it will have nothing to do with racist land-use regulations, and for the Sierra Club, the IWLA, and the Wilderness Society to intervene in some of the cases that are now being heard and some of the litigation that is now going on defending one-acre zoning on the ground that this protects the natural environment."

Wilderness Society to intervene in some of the litigation that is now going on defending one-acre zoning on the ground that this protects the natural environment. It does no such thing. What it protects is the social environment. The conservation organizations should be intervening on the side of some of the smaller-lot zoning and multiple-occupancy housing.

Pankowski: I'm not suggesting that we opt for racist land policies. But I think you will agree that, as long as we allow the proliferation of capital expenditures in shopping centers and in new suburbs, we are drying up the very money that the cities need desperately to rebuild themselves into communities.

Marcuse: I don't think the existing land-use proposals are primarily aimed at that problem.

Hampton: One of the things about the land-use regulations, as applied to construction in the city, is that they are now demanding that HUD only sponsor housing in stable areas where there is a racial mix and an income mix. This means that the hardest pressed areas in the city—the ghettos, which are also the areas nearest downtown—are being neglected. That neglect, in my mind, takes on very systematic proportions. After you get that area totally neglected and it falls into total disuse and abuse, it becomes a no-man's land. Then you bring in that suburban white population that you talked about and move them into a nice new fortress that you construct with moats and guards and chain-link fences and Doberman pinschers—back into the central city, a half-block from their work.

Redus: There's another problem with minorities—those that have recently become journeymen in the construction trades and are now earning the kind of money where they can have a cottage or a boat. The problem is that, now that they can finally get some of the money together to do that, they're told, "No, no, you can't do that. You can't build on the coast any more. We're going to restrict our growth here." Property values go up, so that the house you saw last year for $27,000 is going to cost $40,000. So you just have to go back and work that much harder and save that much more money to try and get out.

Sydney Howe (president, the Conservation Foundation): Peter [Marcuse], I have a reaction to the effect that, at one point, it seems to me you give too much negative credit to the conservationists—I think Ted was saying some of this. However, during the time that the current inner-city condition arose—over quite a long time—the conservation movement wasn't a hill of beans. I do sense, if you mean it more broadly, that perhaps a sort of mixed-up environmental ethic helps create the white noose around so many cities.

In that sense, I can see that maybe the conservation movement has some major role in creating core city problems, but I would have to say that, more accurately, it is the creation of a callous society.

You started off, early on, by saying that perhaps one per cent of the environmental movement would be interested in taking part in the kinds of bridges we have been talking about. I think maybe it was one per cent ten years ago, but I think it's 10 to 15 per cent today. Let's just accept the fact that it's some very small percentage. It seemed to me that you were going on to rather curse that darkness, instead of being willing to light a candle. Those bridges are candles, if they can be built at all.

Marcuse: The point I was trying to make with the one per cent is this: I see, and I throw this out as an uncertain hypothesis, the basis for the alliance between inner-city and conservation as being not the one per cent of the issues presently on the conservation movement's agenda that they can sell to the inner city, but rather being based on the long-range understanding of the conservation movement that its long-range interests have to go with the interests of social justice. What I think this conference could achieve, or what I would see as the specifics, are not so much to bring the one per cent of the issues that are common up to one and a half per cent, but to bring the 10 per cent of the people in the environmental movement to see the long-range importance of a unity of diverse interests up to 20 per cent. To do, in a way, an educational job within the conservation movement.

In Defense of People:
A Thesis Revisited

Reverend Richard Neuhaus
Pastor
St. John the Evangelist Church
Brooklyn, New York

(The following is excerpted from the conference presentation of Mr. Neuhaus, who is the author of *In Defense of People,** a recent book in which he argues that the environmental movement is essentially diversionary because, in his view, it turns public attention away from more pressing requirements for social change.)

SOME OF YOU, I would like to think, are familiar with the thesis of *In Defense of People,* a thesis not uncritical of the environmental movement. I admit to feeling a little like Daniel in the proverbial den. I hope, however, that the ecumenical intent of this meeting, which is the spirit in which Jim [Smith] approached me, will prevail and that, rather than simply an exchange of polemics, we will develop some possible approaches toward collaboration between those thrusts in American life which seem to me to be more directly, more plausibly aimed at the achievement of justice than is the general thrust of the environmental movement.

This has a bearing on my approach to the rhetoric, certainly, and to the substance, I suspect, of much of what is called the environmental movement and the crisis to which it is presumably a response. I am well aware, and have been made more aware by responses to *In Defense of People,* that the "environmental movement" is something of a myth—that, in fact, there are many movements. It is not a monolithic reality. You know that better than I. There are, in some cases, even conflicting thrusts, operating under the banner of environmental or ecological concerns.

Nonetheless, I still suggest it is possible to speak of *an* environmental movement in the sense of a social phenomenon held together by a certain, perhaps minimal, body of concerns and premised upon some common in-

---

* Richard Neuhaus, *In Defense of People* (New York: Macmillan Company, 1971).

junctions regarding the nature of the social crisis in our time—notably, assumptions about the technological nature of our society and the crisis in the resources to maintain that pattern of society. There is a general thrust of suspicion, if not outright hostility, toward technology and especially toward trust in technology; a general suspicion, if not outright hostility, toward most of those things which are the artifacts of human history, notably the cities, and therefore toward much that is associated with the urban history of western civilization. The movement offers, alternatively, a kind of trust in nature; a feeling that somehow we have lost contact with what is genuine, true, and authentic—which is to say, natural—in the human condition and the ordering of human society.

These moods and arguments, I think, characterize what I call the environmental movement.

We can talk about the possibility of building coalitions. I am told that, now, the Wilderness Society and the Sierra Club and—obviously from this meeting—the Conservation Foundation have a desire, which I do not doubt is sincere, to break out, so to speak, of more narrow definitions of what environmentalism is about.

And so we get the rhetoric which says that if you're concerned about the environment, then obviously you're reaching for the whole ball of wax, for we are all products of the environment. Therefore, to be committed to the environmental movement is to be committed to everything—to all that is true and good and beautiful. As rhetoric, this is interesting enough. But obviously, if you're committed to everything, then you really haven't said much of anything. Certainly, you've not urged commitment to anything particular.

Nonetheless, I am sympathetic—I really am—to the desire on the part of many people associated with the environmental movement to relate to the larger picture of social justice. They want to connect environmentalism with the whole question of the reconstruction of our cities, the redistribution of wealth in our society, the anti-war movement, and so forth. And that's encouraging. What is happening comes out of a strange cluster of circumstances which no one fully understands, occurring in the latter part of the '60s when, all of a sudden, the professional environmentalist found himself overwhelmed by popularity. Earth Day, 1970, did not cause it, obviously, but it was a symbol because all of a sudden "the movement" appropriated the environmental movement, also. The various institutions that had for a long, long time been working in the environmental vineyard found their popularity inflated; they had, in most cases, an unwonted influx of interest, membership, etc.

The environmental movement took over when "the movement" had almost gone into receivership. It has arrived at a point at which—especially after '68 and the heightening confrontation in American life symbolized by the Chicago convention which, I think, is probably the symbolic turning

60

point—people wanted to sustain the sense of energetic, perhaps even inevitable, progress; the sense of challenge to the establishment, the kind of metaphor, if you will, that is in Norman Mailer's account of the "armies of the night" and the efforts to levitate the Pentagon. There was something so beautiful, so right about that, that people could stand up against this other myth—the establishment—and somehow not only defy, but overcome.

It was obvious, by the end of the '60s, that the revolution was not happening. People were discouraged, the movement was in disarray, perhaps dead. And then, like a resurrection from the dead, or at least a magic wand that could prolong old life, came Earth Day.

"People realized that maybe we cannot overcome racism in America, and maybe we cannot reconstruct our cities, and maybe we cannot end the war in Vietnam, but, damn it, we can all collect bottles."

Whether or not this desire to perpetuate "the movement" was the major dynamic, it was *a* dynamic and an important one. People realized that maybe we cannot overcome racism in America, and maybe we cannot reconstruct our cities, and maybe we cannot end the war in Vietnam, but, damn it, we can all collect bottles. As James Reston, of the *New York Times*, said the week after Earth Day, "Earth Day was beautiful; it reminded us that we can all do something."

Well, that's history and social analysis in terms of why it came about.

The criticisms of the environmental movement and of the kind of dynamics forged by this unnatural marriage between the movement of the '60s and the environmental movement that I make in *In Defense of People*, I would still, in essence, make today. I've been encouraged, as I indicated, by the number of people—professional people—who have a vested interest, if you will, in promoting the various establishments within the environmental movement. I've been encouraged by the sensitivity and the responsiveness of many of them to the kind of criticism that has been made.

Nevertheless, simply to have someone say that yes, that is a problem, is not really a very effective response to the problem. It doesn't do much about changing the circumstances from which the problem emerged.

I don't know if it is really possible for there to be a coalition between those who earnestly seek social justice and the environmental movement, broadly understood, so long as there are, within this environmental movement, certain pervasive themes, certain ideologies, if you will, deeply rooted, that run counter to the very source and strength of radical politics and of radical moral judgments in social change. I believe, for example—and this is derived not simply from a long Judaeo-Christian tradition of how radical moral challenges are raised in the prevailing order—that such challenges come from the poor.

"New insights and challenges to the status quo emerge along the fault lines of a society. It is along the fault lines of a society that truth is to be discovered — not at the point at which society is successful, but at the point at which society fails."

Historically, this is demonstrable. I think it's an important insight philosophically and even, if you will, theologically, that the genuine thrust of radicalism is aimed at the coming of a new order which, in Biblical metaphor, is the Kingdom of God. This thrust—this discontent with things as they are—emerges from the poor. That is, new insights and challenges to the status quo emerge along the fault lines of a society. It is along the fault lines of a society that truth is to be discovered—not at the point at which society is successful, but at the point at which society fails. The dice of the kingdom are loaded on the side of the poor.

Historically, the environmental movement has, I think, emerged from and been supported by those elements in a society who find the society quite satisfactory, except—of course—that they would prefer more wilderness or whatever for a more secure enclave in nature from the restlessness of history and the demands of the poor. This class factor, which seems to me so much a part of the environmental literature, is a tragic flaw. It is more than simply a strategic difficulty. It is more than a slight oversight which can readily be corrected.

The environmental movement—like any other movement, let me hasten to add—has a kind of symbolic system, a plausibility structure, a world of discourse. Within this world of discourse, there is this element of elitism, evidenced perhaps most odiously and seriously in the attitude toward population growth and the willingness to attribute the problems of poverty to the number of poor people.

In this respect, we see a continuation of a classic conservatism. Conservatism has perennially argued that the primary cause of the problem of poverty is that there are too many poor people. If we could only somehow cut down the number of poor people, it is said, we would be at least along the way toward resolving the problem of poverty.

62

Now, I know that there are grotesque expressions of this viewpoint—at least, in my mind, grotesque. Paul Ehrlich, Hardin, *et al.* People say, "Oh well, when Ehrlich and people like that talk about not only cutting down on population growth, but actually cutting out—or, put less euphemistically, killing—millions of poor people, you have to understand that that's not representative of the environmental movement." I hope that's true. I know many people who are card-carrying members of the environmental movement who find the positions of Ehrlich and Hardin and others as odious as I do. Yet, at the same time, one can't evade the fact that Ehrlich is obviously not a kind of marginal kook in the environmental movement. He is certainly the most sought-after speaker on questions of population control as they relate to the environment and natural resources. His book, *The Population Bomb,* has sold well over two million copies, and it's published by the Sierra Club.

So I am troubled when the people at the top level of the Sierra Club want to disown Ehrlich. One has to ask: is there not something more deeply rooted here? When we are talking about building a coalition between the environmental movement and the quest for social justice, it is not going to be done simply by a strategic pooling of interests. Disagreements touch upon some dramatically conflicting world views.

Last week, at Rutgers University, a group of people very much involved in the environmental movement—a number of professors of ecology and so forth—were discussing how sad it was that a number of benighted folks in the medical disciplines were raising questions about medical ethics in a very awkward way—questions about the definition of life and so forth. They were making the point that we are increasingly moving toward a society that would recognize that there are certain social goods, perhaps even necessities, that require the limitation of the growth of certain kinds of life which are socially non-productive. They were talking about the rights of society to limit the number of births among the very poor, among those who—by genetic research and so forth—could be determined to be defective.

A sociologist said: "Well, that's very strange. You're making some interesting judgments, based on your right to decide what is a quality environment. Is it simply because you have the power, as white, educated, upper-income Americans, to decide what is a quality environment? You toss this phrase, 'quality society,' around as though there'd been some kind of universal referendum on it, or perhaps divine revelation." They insisted that yes, they had that right because they knew best; they knew better than the poor, they knew better than the welfare mothers, and they knew better than the blacks, and so forth, what was a quality environment.

The sociologist suggested: "Well, if you're going to limit the number of children and you have the right to decide, and to push through into law the number of children people can have, why not go to the heart of the problem and, as outrageous as it sounds, simply kill off the welfare mothers?" At this, one professor—of noted ecological wisdom—said, "Well, there are certain social values in our society which would exclude that possibility." But he, being a Parsonian functionalist, was perfectly open to the proposition that social values could be changed. After all, values are like all other institutions.

I see that, to some of you, this exchange seems marginal—and perhaps grotesquely so. But I would suggest that, at the heart of many of the articles and editorials that I have read and continue to read in the mainstream of environmental literature, these types of assumptions about the quality of life and the implicit social policies necessary to achieve it are tossed about in a dangerously mindless way. I would strongly urge that these assumptions be re-examined.

Lynn White, Jr., in his well-known essay about the religious roots of the environmental crisis, talks about the religious assumptions which he feels are to blame for the present environmental crisis—the crucial assumptions being, as he puts it, that human beings have dominion over the earth and that the earth is, in some sense, to be exploited, rather than a home to be nourished and protected.

Whether that's an historically valid thesis (I have my doubts), I think he's on the right track in saying that the environmental movement represents something much more major than an awful lot of people have been willing to allow. It does touch upon certain religious, moral, and philosophical assumptions about the nature of the human condition, the relationship between nature and history, and so forth.

"The values which impel social justice in the Western world . . . are seriously imperiled when, as is frequently done in environmental literature, nature is opposed to history."

I would argue that the values which impel social justice in the Western world—the values which inform the whole ideology of democracy, from the Greek city-states to the Cromwellian revolution and the American Revolution—are seriously imperiled when, as is frequently done in environmental literature, nature is opposed to history. That is, when it is suggested that, somehow, history and human decision-making and politics must be made subservient to natural processes.

This is a very, very dangerous kind of approach, with all kinds of fabulously radical ramifications in terms of social change. What is being suggested, if one takes some of these people seriously, is that the environmental

64

movement represents a revolution of values. Barry Commoner, who seems to me a marvelously sensible and humane individual and sensitive to the dangers of this kind of rhetoric, insists that the environmental movement is really talking about housekeeping.

I agree with him, and I wish that this was reflective of the mainstream, the majority. Indeed, I wish it was reflective of the whole of the environmental movement. However, there are so many who say, "No, we are not satisfied with that. The environmental movement is not simply a matter of housekeeping. It's a question of a whole revolution, a different way of thinking about what it means to be human on this Spaceship Earth."

In terms of the poor, this has tragic consequences, if followed through on. Now I know that, in the last ten years, we have all been treated to very casual and often outrageously mindless allusions to the Third Reich—about how America is like the Third Reich and Nazi-this and Nazi-that. In full awareness, however, of the casual and reckless way in which this comparison is made, I would suggest that the idea that nature—the presumed imperatives of nature—has a role in determining public policy is classically fascist. It was an articulated doctrine of the Nazi regime. It is an articulated doctrine of much of what has been called Western conservatism and of "enlightened" imperialism. It is a kind of social Darwinism—the application to social policies of the biological model of evolution.

It is the old Orwellian thing about how the horse and the chicken are both equal; therefore, the chicken has no room for complaint in the barnyard. The powerful obviously have a built-in advantage. I think this is a reason for concern that is being articulated from the third world today. I was deeply distressed, at the discussion prior to the Stockholm conference, at how many American environmentalists talked—again in their elitist, white, highly developed way—about how the poor of the world didn't understand the nature of the environmental crisis. Many environmentalists seemed not to be very impressed by the truth of what many Asian, African, and Latin American people were saying.

I do not believe that there can be any significant coalition of the search for social justice and environmentalism, as it is presently constituted, unless the latter develops a new kind of sensitivity to those who are outside the sphere of privilege where we can indulge in talk about the dangers of over-technology and of pollution. Those who are outside the charmed circle must be listened to, for according to the basic philosophical premises spelled out before, that is where the truth is being spoken. I think it was General Medici of Brazil who recently said, in his fantastically wild way, "I don't know about all this talk about the environment. What we want is our share of the pollution." In that kind of simplistic statement there is a profound truth that touches on the very nature of justice on our globe.

I don't think that we're going to have, in any facet of this society, a movement for social justice that has real integrity unless we are sensitized in a new way to the injustice in our world; namely, the division between the haves and have-nots, between the undeveloped and developed world, between the first, second, and third worlds, between the north and south of the globe.

The environmental movement, again using this broad category, has been very lax in showing such sensitivity. And, indeed, it has tended to reinforce a dangerous trend in this country that, somehow, we can shed ourselves now of concern about the third world. The trend comes at a dangerous moment, at a moment of meeting with another whole series of developments in America's domestic life. That is, the "after-Vietnam" mentality, even though we're well aware that the war in Vietnam is not over, especially after this past week when more bombs were dropped than in any week of the war.

"Having thoroughly botched the job of being our brother's keeper, we're not even going to try to be our brother's brother."

Nonetheless, this after-Vietnam mentality—some people call it isolationism, but it's more profound—is almost a creed that we can do no good in the rest of the world; that wherever American power touches, it taints; that wherever it tries to help, it only destroys.

And so, having thoroughly botched the job of being our brother's keeper, we're not even going to try to be our brother's brother. This is an increasingly strong feeling in the country now, I think. The environmental movement meets this feeling. It doesn't create it, but it meets it. It says, "Yes, that's right. What we've got to do is clean up our streams and preserve our wilderness and clear our pollution and purify the various foodstuffs and let the rest of the world go by."

Now, again, I realize that all of you can tell me that this is not what you feel, but I hope we can agree that one can find at least the evidences of this kind of feeling and argumentation in much of the environmental literature, public education, propaganda, or whatever we want to call it. It is a very dangerous point of the meeting of moods.

It's extraordinarily dangerous that the American people have been panicked into a survival mentality. The real issue, they have been told, is not to achieve social justice in our society. The real issue is not to rebuild our cities. The real issue is whether we're even going to survive until 1980.

That sounds so nice and radical, so nice and dramatic, but it's also very distracting. There is not much of a difference qualitatively between much of the doomsday rhetoric which characterizes at least a large part of the environmental movement and the doomsday rhetoric on which the Pentagon depends. The Pentagon says that unless we have this missile system or unless we get this appropriation to do such and such, our national security will be imperiled. Anything else we want to do makes no difference whatsoever; this comes first.

"There is not much of a difference qualitatively between much of the doomsday rhetoric which characterizes at least a large part of the environmental movement and the doomsday rhetoric on which the Pentagon depends."

It's tempting when we have a big issue such as the collapse of the ecosystem—that's about as big as you can get—to utilize it for propaganda purposes. I'm surprised at the number of people who are very much involved in environmental circles who are very candid in admitting that, yes, this is what we must do. If not panicked, or at least seriously alarmed, the American people will never get into action. I think it is a very unfortunate strategy, and I think it will backfire. Maybe it has already backfired.

After a while, wolf is cried so often that people are going to turn off to what, in fact, are the very real problems that do need to be attended to in the environment. The Pentagon strategy is also a very, very dangerous policy because, by it, "survival" becomes a prime metaphor in public life. The other considerations which make life human and keep life human fall by the wayside. As a political metaphor, survival is a brutal tyrant.

DISCUSSION

Pankowski: Reverend, you made a statement with respect to the fact that social changes generally come out of the needs of the poor—if I'm paraphrasing it right—and that it has been the poor who have, in effect, been catalyzers of changes in society. If my history is correct, I always thought that movements such as the Magna Carta, the dissolution of the German states by the Junker class, did not come out of those who were concerned with everyday survival. It came out of those who had surplus, in terms of time, money, and energy.

If that is indeed true (and I don't know if it is), then it seems to me that those in our society today, whether they be white, middle-class or otherwise, who have the time, surplus, and energy have the obligation to use that for ends which are not only self-serving. They have the obligation to use the benefits they have received from their position in society to help others. I always thought that was a rather Christian, non-facist point of view.

Neuhaus: Historically, you're quite right in the fact that the middle class has made revolutions. What I hope I said is that the test of truth is along the fault line of society. Those who initiate change are those, indeed, who have options, those who are not struggling every day for simple survival; they must test the truth of that which they do against the needs of the poor. To put it another way, the measure of a society's health, or the measure of the integrity of a movement for change, is the concern it shows for the most vulnerable members of the society.

"It seems to me that what you've done is taken elements out of the environmental literature and environmental rhetoric and, to a certain extent, carried them to the extreme and created a straw man—which is certainly reprehensible and should be condemned."

I wrote *In Defense of People* precisely because the energy for change and the power to effect change is, indeed, in the white, upper-middle class who have, in the last couple of years, become engaged in a kind of environmentalism which is not accountable to the poor. Their truth is not being tested by the fault line.

Paul Swatek (Sierra Club): As I listened to your comments about the environmental movement, I found it difficult to recognize it on the basis of my own everyday, practical experience in New England or, for that matter, in my contact with the national movement. It seems to me that what you've done is taken elements out of the environmental literature and environmental rhetoric and, to a certain extent, carried them to the extreme and created a straw man—which is certainly reprehensible and should be condemned. There are certainly elements of what you see in the movement, but, frankly, I don't see them in the everyday movement as it's implemented.

Part of the environmental movement's basis is ecology, a science with some scientific principles. Part of the ecology movement's underpinnings is the traditional conservation movement, which is based on an ethical system —the land ethic, considerations of the place of man in nature. It's an ethical system with some technical underpinnings.

68

I think you're missing the essence of the environmental movement, as it is actually experienced at the local level. It's a little bit disturbing, as a person who has been involved at the practical level, for me to sit by while this sort of characterization is put forth and enunciated. I think there is a completely different side to the environmental movement—at least from what you said tonight and what I've read in your book—that you've completely missed.

Neuhaus: I think that's a valid criticism, in part. In writing about any social phenomenon, one inevitably tends to deal, perhaps in a disproportionate way, with the literature of the social phenomenon. To that extent, I think it's a valid point. But one has to ask, it seems to me, whether the things that are being said—and being said under unimpeachable environmental-movement auspices—are to be taken seriously.

Scott Paradise said he read my book and realized that much of this could be said about religion. When Bertrand Russell writes, "Why I Am Not a Christian"—which, in recent decades, is a classic polemic against the church—that's helpful, that's good. I think any churchman who is not terribly insecure welcomes that and tries to come to terms with it and see what kind of questions are validly raised there.

If there had been ten other books written, pointing out perhaps what you correctly say—and I hope you're right—are the distortions of the environmental movement, then I would not have written *In Defense of People*. But every movement needs its correctives; it needs constant critique. I only wish that the critique would come more from inside. But it is in the very nature of critique that one does not come down hardest upon the virtues or strong points of the phenomenon you're critiqueing.

Roberts: I was interested in your argument about the conservatism of the environmental movement and philosophy. I gather what you were saying was that this was somehow inherently a contradiction to traditional relations of social justice and the movement in that direction. That strikes me as rather curious. I'd like to ask you to elaborate on it a little more.

Neuhaus: At several points, I would say, there are parallels or corollaries of a classic conservatism. One is the role of nature—that this has priority over the possibility of human decision-making in the search for justice.

Roberts: In what sense does it have priority over human decision-making?

Neuhaus: If one takes the point of reference in the question of population control and the definition of the quality of life. Now that's a very loaded thing. In other words, population control ought to be geared to considerations of the quality of life. A common statement, you will agree?

This assumes some kind of definition regarding the quality of life which, I think—and, again, I've followed Lynn White and Davis and Hardin and others who have spelled this out in greater detail—is readily linked up with notions of a natural order in terms of some selective process within the human community.

Pope: You slip from the biological concept of carrying capacity and say that that leads inevitably to a 19th-century conservative concept of the organic community, with an organic hierarchy.

Who, in the environmental community, is talking in terms of 19th-century organic kinds of hierarchy? You may not like what Hardin does with the question of numbers, but Hardin does not draw hierarchical social conclusions. Hardin has always said that everyone's equal, so I don't think that's hierarchical. I'm not saying I defend it, but I'm saying it's not hierarchical.

Roberts: If you accept the idea that there's a crisis and that the crisis is owing to this population increase and that, to save oneself, you have to somehow limit the population, then you get into this decision of whose population do you limit. How do you decide that?

Neuhaus: Yes, but if you say you limit everyone equally, you begin with the gross inequalities already existing. Therefore, for the people around this room to agree that they're only going to have 1.2 or whatever per mating, and for the people in India to do the same, is not exactly an equal measure, especially in terms of how it would be implemented—namely, one by choice and one by coercion. In fact, it does affirm the natural view.

"Therefore, for the people around this room to agree that they're only going to have 1.2 or whatever per mating, and for the people in India to do the same, is not exactly an equal measure, especially in terms of how it would be implemented—namely one by choice and one by coercion."

In classic Hobbesian conservatism, is it not true that one begins with a kind of large social unit, with a notion of society, if you will? This is a given in classic conservatism. And then one talks about individuals and individual groups and so forth in terms of serving that social order. That's the ecological concept called society . . .

Roberts: That's not at all Hobbes . . .

Neuhaus: . . . It is, in fact, that the natural warfare must be controlled and limited in terms of the larger welfare and its prime goal, which is society. I would say that, in the environmental movement, you have an even more extreme position than that—you not only take society, but you take a real mythological construction—the ecosystem, or Spaceship Earth.

70

Pope: I will submit that you may not understand it, but it is not a mythological construction. An ecosystem is not a myth.

Neuhaus: By myth, I do not mean something that is false. I do not mean it does not exist. A myth is an ordering model or it may, in some cases, even be a demonstrable truth. But it is a basic model from which you begin conceptually.

Borrelli: I don't think one can conclude that, with this so-called moral basis to the movement, one has to fear the distant sound of hob-nailed boots. I see anything but fascist overtones to it—even in the extremes of its literature. I see anything *but* a mistrust of social order. I think, at the basis of it, that the primary tenets of it are an affinity for nature that allows us, if you will, to do our housekeeping in a much better way; an affinity with nature that allows us to be more critical of our social institutions and our government, in particular with regard to how we go about our daily housekeeping.

I think that's where we're at, if we're anywhere. I don't believe we're at a stage where a movement has been defined. If anything, we are at that springboard stage at which people are seeking a certain commonality of spiritual or moral ordering of values.

Neuhaus: I think that's very, very useful. I don't hear hob-nailed boots echoing, except in some of the literary allusions. I don't hear them in the environmental movement as I've experienced it.

At the same time, what was said about the truth to be discovered in the pines and what Barry Goldwater has frequently said about worshiping in the "Cathedral of the Pines" are strikingly similar. When one looks again at much of the literature—especially creeds popularized by the environmental movement, John Muir literature, and so on—the preachment is pervasive

---

"I don't think one can conclude that, with this so-called moral basis to the movement, one has to fear the distant sound of hob-nailed boots. I see anything but fascist overtones to it—even in the extremes of its literature. I see anything but a mistrust of social order."

---

that, somehow, truth is to be discovered apart from people, that the city is dirty, the city is corrupt, the artifacts are false. One meets God apart from the city—pre-eminently the city, which is the very epitome of everything contrary to God's will. This is a theme that, like a trip hammer, goes through much of the literature of conservation. I think you all recognize that.

71

Can we feel this same sense of the sacred with regard to the Williamsburg section of Brooklyn and the blacks and Puerto Ricans where I live and work?

When one creates a climate which, it seems to me, much of the environmental movement is helping to create, in which it is thought that truth and purity and the good are to be discovered in turning away from technology, away from urbanization, away from those things which somehow have gone sour, then that's a very dangerous climate quite beyond personal sensibilities. In terms of public climate, I think we need to create a new sense of adventure about the urban enterprise and about the reconstruction of our inevitably urbanized society along patterns of justice.

I hope that, regardless of our individual clusters of sensibilities, we can agree that that is an urgent item in terms of the public mood.

CHAPTER V

The Double Standard of Open Space

Charles E. Little
Senior Associate
The Conservation Foundation
Washington, D. C.

THE CHALLENGE, "environmental quality for whom?", as it is often and somewhat stridently put, is an important one to be addressed not only by those who consider themselves environmentalists, but by everyone who has an interest in the philosophical underpinnings of democracy. Looking at this challenge from various angles, the picture is not altogether bleak. There are three basic elements of the biophysical environment whose quality we would improve. For two of these elements, air and water, it is difficult for erroneous assumptions, selfish motives, or even stupidly conceived programs to result in malapportionment of the fruits of even minimal reform. We all breathe the air; we all drink the water. This generalization is, of course, not without certain kinds of exceptions at the micro-scale, but until someone figures out how to manipulate the planetary spin to affect prevailing winds or to cause water to flow in some manner other than downhill, the gross tendency is toward an egalitarian distribution of the benefits of improved water quality and improved air quality.*

That was the good news. The bad news is that this tendency does not hold in respect to the third basic element of the biophysical environment—the land. Unfortunately, the land is stationary; it does not move across the visual or experimental field. Mahomet goes to the mountain, and so must non-Mahomets in search of land quality. The trouble is that ours is not a society in which Mahometan mobility is equally distributed.

---

* To the extent that the less affluent tend to live downwind and downstream, air and water improvement may have greater benefits for them. However, the cost of pollution cleanup may, unless legislated otherwise, be borne disproportionately by the poor. If costs are passed along to consumers, price increases become, in effect, a regressive tax.

Moreover, landscape quality, which is to say whatever obtains in respect to the natural or built environment at ground zero, tends to elude Americans altogether as physical dimension having its own set of intrinsic values subject to law and equity. Our theory of land-as-commodity may be due to what one might call a "frontier expectation" deeply ingrained in our consciousness. Those island forebears, the English, have had no such problem. The finitude of their land mass has produced not only rigorous national constraints on land use, but also what may pass as a level of national

---

"The literature of parks and open space is filled with pieties ranging from Olmstedian fervor for urban uplift, through crude explanations of the 'balance of nature,' to the most recent rhetoric of the federal government about 'parks to the people.' Therefore, 'environmental quality for whom?,' in respect to landscape deserves analysis, and most especially in terms of parks and open space, since our objectives here are ostensibly democratic."

"taste" in natural beauty—a sensitivity to landscape quality.[1] The U.S. policy of land use mainly for economic gain, with one exceptional aspect, characterizes our decision-making process, and constitutes one of the few remaining opportunities for complete scoundrels to enrich themselves with impunity at the public expense.

The blessed though paltry exception to this policy is a national penchant for parks and open space. What is curious about this singular acknowledgment of landscape for other than economic values is that its political justification is not primarily a matter of "taste" or aesthetics, but rather of egalitarian public service, having to do with recreational opportunity and, to a lesser extent, ecological "balance" as a subsidiary rationale. The literature of parks and open space is filled with pieties ranging from Olmstedian fervor for urban uplift, through crude explanations of the "balance of nature," to the most recent rhetoric of the federal government about "parks to the people." Therefore, "environmental quality for whom?", in respect to landscape deserves analysis, and most especially in terms of parks and open space, since our objectives here are ostensibly democratic.

74

I

Park and open-space programs operate in three geographical contexts: city, suburb, and wilderness—the last term being used here to stand for relatively unmanaged scenic landscapes at a discontinuous remove from metropolitan agglomerations. In these contexts, park and open-space efforts can be described as an institutional reflection of the principal means by which urban man has historically engaged in the Edenic search.[2] He has, since the beginnings of civilization, sought gardens in his cities, a pastoral landscape outside of his cities, and wilderness for retreat away from his cities. Baghdad boasted a thousand gardens; Alexander set aside one quarter of his north African city as a park; Virgil, a Roman, and Theocritus, a Greek, are credited with the literary initiation of the pastoral ideal; wilderness served as retreat for Jesus of Nazareth, as it did later for the Waldensians and the Franciscans; and meditation in the wilderness is a common theme in Far Eastern cultures.

Thus, there is good evidence that a propensity for greenery as a substitute Eden in urban civilizations is not a peculiarity of any single race, religion, or national culture. To be sure, the English have developed a pastoral aesthetic in their planning policies to a greater degree than most; Americans, and people in some Northern European countries, have a fondness for accessible wilderness; and the Japanese have developed small-space garden design to a high art. But the historical evidence seems to indicate a certain universality in the human desire for gardens, pastoral landscapes, and wilderness that can serve as the necessary contrast to the urban milieu.

In its application in the U.S., this park and open-space imperative has become slightly skewed. Instead of resting on the historical evidence of universality, the allocation of greenery in the U.S. tends to increase with wealth and with the proportion of Northern Europeans to the total population. Our policies seem to be based on the assumption that poor people, especially blacks and Latins, do not even *like* greenery, except maybe watermelon rinds and plantain leaves. The logic of our policy seems to rest on this syllogism: inner cities have no greenery; poor people live in inner cities; therefore parks, open space, and wilderness are not necessary for them. City park budgets shrink, the disenfranchised are barred from suburbia, and National Park tourism policies tend to exclude the non-affluent.

That there is no historical evidence to support a double standard of parks and open space for certain races or social classes does not seem to make much difference at this point, for the burden of proof has been subtly shifted from the opponents of greenery for the poor to the proponents. They have been asked to prove the obvious in order to refute a fallacy. In the 1966 Senate hearings on the federal role in urban affairs, the Institute for Public Administration did, in fact, attempt such proof by introducing a

75

revealing survey (conducted by John F. Kraft, Inc.) [3] which measured the attitudes of Harlem residents toward their own blocks. Each respondent was asked what he liked *least* about the block. The list was headed by absence of greenery:

Not enough trees and grass	24%
Not enough policemen	15%
Bad services in the building	13%
Need more projects, tear down slums	9%
Tough kids, dangerous	7%
People fighting	7%
Building unsafe	6%
(Other complaints not enumerated)	

There are surveys that may produce inferences at variance with this one. However, there is enough evidence here, one hopes, to refute any simple-minded assumption that all residents of Harlem, say, are by virtue of race and location somehow constitutionally unwilling and unable to appreciate natural surroundings.

Such a fallacy, however persuasively it may be challenged, is nevertheless likely to continue. Its expression in policy, whether intentional or not, may be useful to examine in the hope that such policies may be capable of change.

II

The open-space double standard begins in the city. In most big cities there are, to be sure, large parks—such as Central Park in New York, or Golden Gate Park in San Francisco, or Rock Creek Park in Washington, D. C. These, and satellite parks, are quite adequate on their own terms. The problem is that their terms are irrelevant to most of those who now live in cities.

Central Park, a replica of idealized English landscape, is (except for a swimming pool) virtually deserted at its northern end (in contrast to the more heavily used area to the south). The dense neighborhood that borders the northern end is Harlem. The conclusion is therefore drawn that blacks have no interest in, or need for, community open spaces. Such a simple conclusion fails to differentiate between green space and social space.*

A few years ago, the magazine *Open Space Action* interviewed a nine-year-old Puerto Rican boy named Sergio. Sergio lived in the South Bronx. It turned out that Sergio had never been to Central Park, just a few miles away, and in fact had never been to *any* park. When the idea of "park" was described to him, he said that the *street* where he lived was his park.[4]

---

* I use this term in the sense of discrete, physical space in which to socialize, rather than the broader definition used by some geographers.

76

Edward Hall, the anthropologist, reports that in Chicago the basic areal unit in black neighborhoods is the block. Not only is it the block, but often a *single side* of one or, at most, two blocks. "The informal communal enclave," says Hall, "first developed in rural communities. This same organization was later transferred to the city where it managed to remain viable on blocks with separate houses and was even able to adapt to the row house and low-rise apartments centered on a court or mews." [5]

"Our policies seem to be based on the assumption that poor people, especially blacks and Latins, do not even like greenery, except maybe watermelon rinds and plantain leaves."

Findings such as this have been frequent lately, and the idea of community territoriality has been vigorously communicated to urban redevelopers. The notion has not been apprehended by park planners, however, for the assumption has held that a park a few blocks away—whether it is Central Park or a vacant lot—should provide both green space *and* social space. Since community boundaries in poor neighborhoods tend to be highly restricted, a park two streets over may serve no better as social space than a park in the next state.

In poor urban neighborhoods, the street is the social space. This space is as private, in its way, as the suburban back yard. The assumption that city dwellers do not want or need social space, or that parks provide some kind of substitute, is in error. Streets are, in fact, the habitation grounds of the city neighborhood, just as much as the yards of suburbia are habitation grounds. The concept of semi-private social space—i.e., turf—is not purely urban; it is a universal condition. The substitution of parks for social space is a serious error in planning, and one which is hardly mitigated by elaborate recreational programs in larger parks, or even by trying, here and there, to convert vacant lots into mini-parks. Instead, city dwellers are criticized for using streets as commons ("Look at those children playing in the street!") and for not sharing the planners' confusion between green space and social space ("They just don't appreciate parks; why, they hardly use them at all!").

Failing to perceive how open-space resources could be appropriately allocated to those living in dense urban areas, the proponents of parks and open space have concentrated on the suburbs as a suitable place to provide acreage to "the metropolitan area as a whole." Thus, the greatest part of new park and open-space land has ended up in a ring around the cities

77

rather than distributed within them. The pious assumption has been that poor people were not necessarily barred from such facilities; that they had every bit as much right to them as anyone else; that this right could be exercised simply by coming to the Land of Open Space for a visit, or by moving themselves to the suburbs.

While there are some suburban parks that receive heavy use by urban visitors, the overall patronage of most such areas by poor non-residents is so small that this egalitarian assumption can hardly be put to the test. The poor, especially the black, hardly feel welcome in suburbia, even for a day trip. Moreover, of the 25 per cent of Americans who own no personal automobile, a virtually essential precondition for use, the largest part are the urban poor and elderly.

"Central Park . . . is virtually deserted at its northern end. . . . The conclusion is therefore drawn that blacks have no interest in, or need for, community open space. Such a simple conclusion fails to differentiate between green space and social space."

But the worst aspect of the open-space double standard has nothing to do with parks at all. It has to do with the systematic residential exclusion of the poor and minorities from the "lovely green hollows" of suburbia. Suburbia's spaciousness is as much a draw for the poor and minorities as it is for everyone else. Market surveys of black families wishing to move out of the ghetto show that these families have the same aspirations as whites. They want single-family houses on individual lots, together with all the services and amenities that the suburbs provide.[6]

Yet the assumption prevails that such an environment is of no interest to such families, since they do not tend to settle there. The facts are that suburban housing, typically costing $35,000 per unit in the suburbs, is simply unaffordable to those families whose earnings are $17,000 a year or less. This describes 90 per cent of the black population.[7]

The remaining setting in which the double standard operates is in our national parks. Again, the instinct to preserve land as part of the "national estate" suggests an egalitarian impulse which, on the face of it, should not be questioned. But here, too, the poor and minority groups tend not to be legatees of this estate. For a variety of reasons, among them difficulties of transportation, lack of sufficient discretionary income, as well as the

78

sense of "not belonging," the national parks' user profile is primarily middle—to upper middle—income. For example, 1968 figures show that those with less than a high-school education comprise 44 per cent of our population, but only 26.6 per cent of National Park users; those with an income of less than $5,000 comprise 30.8 per cent of the population but only 18.6 per cent of Park users; and those who are non-white comprise 13.2 per cent of our 18-and-over population, but only 4.4 per cent of Park users.[8]

III

Surprisingly, few in our society seem even to be aware that the malapportionment of open space is, in fact, unjust. Open space may be such a low-priority issue as a component of both environmentalism and social justice that no one cares to examine it closely.

"Streets are . . . the habitation grounds of the city neighborhood, just as much as the yards of suburbia are habitation grounds. The concept of semi-private social space—i.e., turf—is not purely urban; it is a universal condition."

There are some, however, who believe that open space, whether in the form of parks, gardens, a pastoral environment, or wilderness, may be a vital component for life, liberty, and the pursuit of happiness, and that, for this reason, the injustice of the double standard should be seriously addressed and remedial planning constructs developed.

Let us imagine, for a minute, some scenarios that might accomplish a more equitable distribution of public open space in America and, at the same time, a more humane environment for all. Beginning in the cities, a distinction should be drawn between a street and a road. The former is for people, while the latter is for vehicles, as architectural critic Wolf Von Eckardt has pointed out.[9] Sometimes, in cities, the roads are called avenues. Therefore, the distinction should be made between streets and those avenues that operate as thoroughfares. Streets should then be considered as grounds and landscaped appropriately for such a use, not for cars. Paving should be in earth-colored garden stone; there should be beds for flowers and shrubs and vegetables. Some of the street should be in grass. It is fun to play on, and besides, it's soft and cool. Elsewhere on the block, swings and a basketball hoop should be installed, just as in the yards of suburbia. Trees should be plentiful—for shade and quiet and color. Vines should be used for the same purpose on walls and outdoor architecture. Benches and chairs should be plentiful for sitting down, for getting to know your neighbors. The maintenance manpower for these former streets should be provided by former traffic cops.

Because a street should serve a basic *social* function, the park, which might be two blocks away—or ten—should truly provide a contrast from busy city life; it should not be judged a failure if it is not absolutely swarming with happy natives. The park should contain some large recreational playing fields, swimming pools and similar facilities, to be sure,

---

> *". . . the worst aspect of the open-space double standard has nothing to do with parks at all. It has to do with the systematic residential exclusion of the poor and minorities from the 'lovely green hollows' of suburbia."*

---

but it should, for the most part, consist of what is most commonly called today a "passive-use natural area." The woodlands should be representative of the biotype, with spring peepers heralding the new season, with plenty of raccoons and possums. Birds should be plentiful in the parks, with streamside trails producing the sighting of a spotted sandpiper, tail awag on a wet log, or, less often, a little green heron. At the meadow's edge, the warbler fancier should be able to check off five or ten different species on his list in a morning. The woodland paths should be pleasant, quiet, though the city park rangers would often be encountered on the trails, keeping them free of refuse or, alternatively, explaining to a youngster how the Indians made arrows from the viburnum now called arrowwood. The city park rangers—a large and elite corps—should be former policemen who have been retained as naturalists.

How wild is the vision? Not very. There are a few such streets in inner cities today—or at least streets that approach such a description. And there are a few such parks, or at least areas of parks.

If the suburbs were the preference—and they would have to be actually preferred, for in this vision there would be fewer reasons for those who are truly urban to leave the city—then the poor man as well as the rich should be able to find a genuine pastoral landscape aesthetic, as proposed in 2,000 years of literature. Instead of the seemingly endless sprawls we now know, suburbs should be villages, composed of a series of hamlets, closely spaced, that together make up a village and support the services a village can provide. The houses should be unprepossessing, and by and large fitted into the landscape through the architectural idea of geomancy. In China, this concept is called *feng-shui,* defined according to geographer Yi-Fu Tuan as "the art of adapting the residences of the living and the dead so as to co-operate and harmonize with the local currents of the cosmic breath." [10]

Natural materials should be used for the structures; there should be very little formal landscaping associated with the dwellings, which should be artfully built into rocky slopes or rolling wooded areas in ways that

---

"Beginning in the cities, a distinction should be drawn between a street and a road. The former is for people, while the latter is for vehicles, as architectural critic Wolf Von Eckardt has pointed out."

---

will permit considerable density but produce near-perfect quiet and privacy. The density should be such that quite a few families can live in such villages: the land mass of suburbia is now so great that all who wish to live there may do so. And yet the diameter of the metropolitan areas as a whole need be no greater than it would be under our present practice of each family owning more land than it can afford or maintain. Some people might choose to own sizeable single-family dwelling lots, but they would be in the minority. To live there would be neither as convenient, as efficient, nor as aesthetically attractive as living in hamlet communities.

The village may, within its political boundaries, contain, say, eight square miles, but only three square miles should be developed. The average density of the developed areas should be five dwelling units per acre. The village would have a population, then, of about 35,000. Five square miles should be field and forest, mountain and river. Lovely green hollows should abound and be an intimate part of the everyday life of all who live there. The five square miles should, of course, link up with the open spaces of neighboring villages in a linear fashion which leaves undisturbed and undeveloped the major landscape features, including the principal drainage ways, the ridgelines of hills, and outstanding scenic areas. The village should own all this land. Much of it should be put to agricultural or silvicultural use on a lease basis. The fine old houses should be kept as dwellings for the professional farmers and foresters, and for public recreational and cultural purposes. Many of the prospects, the striking visual landscapes, may once have been sites for those 1950s-style subdivisions of half-acre, single-family houses. They should be razed. The land should be reclaimed and legally bound as "forever pastoral."

Impossible to achieve? Perhaps, but this is the vision of open-space (as opposed to "park") planners, such as Ian McHarg,[11] as well as a few new-town and new-community planners.

Wherever you live in this visionary egalitarian metropolis of green, on the garden street of the city or within the bucolic landscape of the suburbs, you might decide some winter night that you are going to take that month's vacation owed you and get into some real wilderness, for even the garden life of the city or the pastoral life of the suburbs is not without its tensions and its visual and social anomalies. You would then reserve space on the park train. It would be possible to drive, of course, but too expensive, too time-consuming, and too complicated. The park train, a public conveyance financed in part by the National Park Service,

---

"Because a street should serve a basic social function, the park, which might be two blocks away — or ten — should truly provide a contrast from busy city life; it should not be judged a failure if it is not absolutely swarming with happy natives."

---

just as subways are subsidized by city governments, will perhaps turn out to be the best way ever devised to get an idea of the vastness and the grandeur of the American land. En route, people will tell you over and over that, even if there weren't a national park to get off at, the train ride would be worth it, just to see the country rushing by the windows. Once arrived at the park, you would be able to pitch your tent in a camping area if you were the neighborly type, or have it packed in for you along with the rest of the supplies you need to get to more remote spots. If tenting is not your style, you would perhaps choose one of the primitive-area camps, which you could reach by hiking, horseback, or jeep trail for those unable to make it otherwise. At a primitive-area camp, park personnel would be on hand to provide meals and other services, but most importantly you would be under the tutelage of a specially trained "program ranger" who would instruct you in the ways of the back country. If you are the exceptionally hardy type, probably you would prefer the real wilderness, which would be wholly protected from any incursion of civilization, no matter how tentative. There would be trails and designated camp sites, but nothing else between you and the timeless land, whether it be a lonely island beach or a rugged mountain. In any case, you would look in vain

82

for exclusive and intimidating resort accommodations, tawdry gateway communities, trinket shops, and Winnebago parking hookups. If these were your pleasure, you would be advised at the National Park and Forest Information Center in the city that perhaps a commercial resort area might be more agreeable. The wilderness doesn't care who enjoys it, but the experience should be on its terms, not those of exclusionary industrial tourism catering only to the tastes of affluent Americans.

Too visionary? The scenario above is, with only a few embellishments, based on the recommendations of the Conservation Foundation to the National Park Centennial Commission. This year-long study involved over two hundred citizens, of all kinds, who visited the parks and made their views known in task forces and at a symposium in Yosemite National Park in the spring of 1972.

So goes a sampling of some truly egalitarian park and open-space visions—of the city, of the suburbs, of our wilderness and near-wilderness areas. They are not original. But visions such as these are too faintly proposed by environmentalists. The reasons for this are complex, but illustrative of the ambiguities of environmentalism in today's society. To assume that it is mainly because environmentalists are bigoted, self-absorbed, and jealous of class prerogatives is to fall into the same snares of logic that have led to unequal open-space distribution in the first place. What is more likely is that environmentalists have failed to distinguish between a superficial ad hoc reaction to landscape destruction and the need for an affirmative policy of reform. Should an open-space reform policy ever reach a rough consensus among environmentalists, those elements of the movement—so distasteful to many liberals—who seem to be using the open-space issue to stop social progress in its tracks would be purged by their own hand. For a truly egalitarian open-space policy would not only be an effective means to improve landscape quality, it would also reveal itself, surely, as a potent weapon in the struggle to achieve a decent, human, and dignified way of life for those Americans who have thus far been denied it.

NOTES TO CHAPTER FIVE

1. David Lowenthal and Hugh C. Prince, "English Landscape Tastes" in *Man, Space, and Environment*. ed. Paul Ward English and Robert C. Mayfield. New York: Oxford University Press, 1972, pp. 81-112.

2. This concept is developed more fully in Charles E. Little, *A Town is Saved . . .* New York: Sierra Club Books, 1973. See also Clarence J. Glacken, "Man's Place in Nature in Recent Western Thought," in *This Little Planet*, ed. Michael Hamilton, New York: Charles Scribner's Sons, 1970. Glacken, *Traces on a Rhodian Shore*, Berkeley: University of California Press, 1967. Leo Marx, *The Machine in the Garden*, New York: Oxford University Press, 1972 (Galaxy Books edition). Roderick Nash, *Wilderness and the American Mind*, New Haven: Yale University Press, 1971. Paul Shepard, *Man in the Landscape*, New York: Ballantine Books, 1972.

3. Reported in Whitney North Seymour's, "An Introduction to Small Urban Spaces," *Small Urban Spaces*, ed. Whitney North Seymour, New York: New York University Press, 1969. pp. 7-8.

4. "Breaking the Space Barrier," *Open Space Action*. Oct.-Nov. 1968. p. 16.

5. Edward T. Hall. "Environmental Communication" in *Behavior and Environment*, ed. Aristede H. Esser, New York-London: Plenum Press, 1971. p. 251-2.

6. Donald L. Foley, "Institutional and Contextual Factors Affecting the Housing Choices of Minority Residents," in *Segregation in Residential Areas*, ed. Amos H. Hawley and Vincent P. Rock, Washington, D. C., National Academy of Sciences, 1973. p. 92.

7. Linda and Paul Davidoff and Neil Gold, "The Suburbs Have to Open Their Gates," *New York Times Magazine*, November 7, 1971.

8. Statistics from Department of the Interior as quoted in Doris Y. Wilkinson, "The Class Imperative: the 'Greening' and 'Blueing' of America." *National Parks for the Future*, Washington, D. C.: The Conservation Foundation, 1972. p. 240-241.

9. Wolf Von Eckardt, "The New Urban Vision," Lecture to the American Association for the Advancement of Science, December 27, 1972. Mimeographed. For a comparison of European street use with the American, see Bernard Rudofsky, *Streets for People*, New York: Doubleday and Company, 1969.

10. Yi-Fu Tuan, "Our Treatment of the Environment in Ideal and Actuality," *Ekistics* 198 (May, 1972) p. 401.

11. See especially Ian McHarg, *Design with Nature*, Garden City, New York: The Natural History Press, 1969. The section "Response to Values" (pp. 79-93) describes McHarg's remarkable "Plan for the Valleys" which expresses the pastoral mode in suburban planning terms. The rationale for the plan is, however, ecological, rather than wholly aesthetic.

CHAPTER VI

Dialogue: Metropolitan Growth and Inner-City Survival

I. Transportation—*Angela Rooney*
National Coalition for the Transportation Crisis
Washington, D. C.

II. Housing—*Morton Isler*
The Urban Institute
Washington, D. C.

III. Employment—*Wayne Redus*
Human Rights Commission of San Francisco
San Francisco, California

I. Transportation

Angela Rooney: I feel a tremendous responsibility here because I come as a private citizen. I work with people who work out of their kitchens and church basements, and who are down at city hall every day of their lives. It's a tough fight. It's very nice to do a little soul-searching and worry about the cosmic impacts. However, I would like to be as practical as possible.

Let me start with the proposition that the urban freeway system, as it has operated and still operates, has been a tool of both social injustice and environmental destruction.

Our transportation policy has been completely dominated for 20 years by the Federal-Aid Highway Act and the Highway Trust Fund. Practically all major land-use changes and development in our cities and suburbs have come through the initial thrust of where these big roads will go. Even though 50 per cent of our adult population does not or cannot drive, every other form of ground transportation has been practically relegated to the junk heap. We now conceive, live, bank, shop, attend church, seek entertainment—and are frequently killed—in our automobiles.

As the Trust Fund, over the years, has swelled with more and more money, Detroit's part of the bargain was kept and it furnished the cars that built the roads that created the jams that demanded the new roads. State highway officials are asking for $350 *billion* by 1985. I bring all of this in because there is kind of a myth abroad that, "Gee, they're beginning to stop all these freeways." It ain't so, at all!

On top of this great big public trough, with the politicians drinking heavily, we have the mayors and the governors and the planners and the architects setting up a system of favors and grants and jobs that take care of dispensing the 90-10 money or the 70-30 or the 50-50 money. Underneath that came what we call urban planning. It is pretty much nonsense.

We have all seen, over and over again, how the urban freeway has devastated the inner city. And because we're talking about social justice, I would like to mention one specific case where a freeway was identified by the first Secretary of Transportation, Alan Boyd, as going through the black residential community because it had no political clout. It was that simple. The freeway had originally been intended to go through the white affluent section of Washington, D. C. They couldn't get it through. In fact, the people were powerful enough to write a law in Congress that no freeway be built west of Rock Creek Park.

So the highway lobby simply went after a more vulnerable part of the city, attempting to blast right through Northeast Washington.

This kind of wholesale destruction of community identification and political strength took place in almost every major city in the country. Now, as I said yesterday, we used the phrase which was absolutely accurate for that situation and many others, that these were "white men's roads through black men's homes." This was true because, in destroying the political clout of the community, you make the rest of the land-taking like cutting butter. If a community cannot resist the impact of a 10- or 12-lane freeway, they can't resist anything else either. They've been had!

The flight from the city to the suburbs was based on many things, but it was certainly facilitated and encouraged by the interstate freeway system and major highway networks. As we fled the cities for the suburbs, we are now fleeing the suburbs for the outer beltways, and we are fleeing the outer beltways for our second house in Paradise Valley, and they are all touted as being tantalizingly close by a freeway.

Cities now devote almost 50 per cent of their land to the care, feeding, storing, and moving of automobiles. All this is lost to the tax rolls. Ninety per cent of the air is heavy with carbon monoxide, lead, nitrous oxide, zinc, cadmium, and particulate matter that comes from the cars. And this is just the tip of the iceberg. We haven't even begun to really measure the full impact. Countless businesses and jobs have been lost. I say countless because it was not possible for the Department of Transportation—even the section ostensibly responsible for developing the statistics on the socio-economic effects of freeway construction—to give any figures at all on the numbers of businesses that have been displaced or lost outright, or jobs that

86

were lost to the community by freeway construction. Nor were they available from the Department of Labor, the Department of Commerce, the Senate Government Operations Committee, or the federal Office of Management and Budget.

I think it's important to note how many businesses are lost in our cities and in our suburbs by freeway construction, and how many jobs lost are absent from the calculations of those who determine our transportation policy.

There's a study coming out which does not yet have a name. It was made by the Civil Rights Commission and finished in the summer of 1972. It's a report on the discriminatory effects of the Federal-Aid Highway program, and it will deal with jobs and housing and what actually has happened to the poorer communities—particularly black communities—in our cities. I hope that people will get it as soon as it comes out. It also bears on the economic cost of urban freeways. I will mention very briefly the statistics on housing, because that is a 1:2 ratio: two million housing units lost, one million supposedly replaced.

As more and more cities are losing their communities of homeowners and residents who have a sense of identification with a particular neighborhood, they have become the playgrounds of the upward-mobile, affluent, expense-account crowd who really couldn't care less about community responsibility, or they have become the refuge of the poor who, in a very real way, are *denied* responsibility for their community.

It has been driven home, in more ways than one, that the freeways serve as the buffers between the obviously incompatible forces who now remain in our cities. The Lower Manhattan Expressway was planned to serve this function between the development of Battery Park and the rather "undesirable" elements who held sway in Greenwich Village. It is supposed to take place in Washington, D. C., by the construction of the North Leg, which would keep the federal city more or less intact, and allow it to be returned to the upward-mobile, affluent, temporary dwellers, separating them from the still remaining, largely black north area.

It may not be an exaggeration to say that very little development of *any* size has been conceived in our cities in the last 20 years that has not been firmly dependent upon automobile traffic.

The highway planners and builders can be very cynical in the way they attempt to manipulate the citizen. For example, there is a study called "the Larrabee Report." It was issued by the Federal Highway Administration to all state highway officials and has been put into practice, believe me, showing how you take the basic [Saul] Alinsky theory of organizing citizens and turn it around to organize the citizens for the purposes of building new freeways. It completely coöpts citizen effort. It buys them off, it intimidates them, it deceives them and, in the end, as the study concludes, the public hearing is only a matter of form, a "ritual" without any meaning.

Another way to build the freeway against the interests and will of the people is to declare an area urban-renewable—by concluding that "this area is so bad that we're going to just clean it up and reconstruct the whole thing." When the dust from the wrecking crew clears, you have a freeway, and you have some developers having a marvelous time operating from some freshly cleared land. It is control and exploitation at government expense.

A third way is for a combination of government agencies and private corporations to construct a "magnet" that will induce so much heavy traffic that building a road becomes a necessity. This is a very popular gimmick. Right now, with the Bicentennial coming up, every tired old plan for a sports arena, civic center, or parking plaza that the citizens have kicked out will be dusted off and brought out again. "We've got to have it for the Bicentennial. We must be proud of our city."

Last but not least, the highway lobby has the power to control Congress, when it's being blocked by citizens and the courts, and force legislation that will read, in part, as it did in the last Highway Act: "No court shall have power or authority to issue any order or to take any action which will, in any way, impede, delay or halt the construction of . . ."

We've been talking primarily about the cities, but what about the rest of the country? Surely we have learned something from the mess we see in our cities and the recognition that the same thing is beginning to take place in our suburbs. Some 200 lawsuits against the Department of Transportation would seem to indicate the need for a change in transportation policy. But not hardly.

In the 1970 Highway Act, Section 127 provides for a demonstration program for "economic growth center development highways," with a modest starter of $100 million. It is really a blanket proposal to speed up existing road proposals that have been dragging behind schedule, as well as to create a gigantic network of roads, with new economic centers wherever big business would like to have them. Under the public relations motto of helping rural America, the program would actually wipe out the business centers of small towns all over, and center the action on where the big roads intersect in giant shopping centers or industrial parks. This was discussed in depth in the October, 1972 *CF Letter*.

In a way, this is really one of the biggest land grabs since the opening of the West. This tentative program, in 1970, was hardly noticed except by certain governors and mayors and the highway lobby. Within a very few months, Volpe had approved 98 "economic growth development center highway" programs, and the citizens who were involved and were going to be displaced, and the cities that were going to be totally changed by the impact of a superimposed road network, didn't know anything about it.

These things move very fast, and so—as the freeway culture has dominated our cities—it is absolutely set up to dominate the rest of the

88

country. The only practical way to bring it under control is to cut off the money. If the Highway Trust Fund is not abolished, it should at least be opened wide and totally restructured to meet the needs of the people through referenda at the local level.

DISCUSSION

Stewart Brandborg (Executive Director, the Wilderness Society): What you encountered in the bureaucracy of the Highway Administration is exactly what the Wilderness Society has faced when it works with the Department of the Interior or the Department of Agriculture in wilderness preservation, or in trying to stave off an environmentally destructive pipeline in Alaska that is pushed by the oil corporations. This is typical of goverment everywhere. I think, without going into a lot of other issues, you have given us one that has the basic elements of most of the problems that we face.

Morton Isler (Director of Housing Studies, the Urban Institute): One thought I had during your talk was that it is very clear that the people who are proponents of highways have a great deal of technical resources and professional resources at their bidding. This is really a critical part of the problem. I don't think that it is probably as true in the conservation area. A lot of the highway issues are very difficult to study. I'm talking about a specific issue there that Mr. Norton could tell us about—the Lower Manhattan Expressway. I was in New York when that issue was developing, and I would disagree with what you said about that.

There were people who felt—and, again, there were no people who really did good objective analysis—that the Lower Manhattan Expressway would link the Brooklyn industrial areas, which were important sources of employment for lower-income people living in Bedford-Stuyvesant and places like that, to the rest of the region. The decision, I think, was heavily based on very local opposition to the Expressway in lower Manhattan, even though it really affected the lives of possibly a million people living in Brooklyn. To be positive about it, what I am saying is it takes a level of technical resources (a) that can't be entrusted to government, and (b) that citizens just don't have.

Rooney: It is not easy to come by *pro bono* help, but we're finding more and more professional people who are willing to do public-interest work. This is what we need, and we need a lot more of it. But don't forget that the highway departments and planners would love nothing better than to think that citizens couldn't understand the plans. And, from the point of view of the citizen and his stake in the community's survival, the "experts" don't always know what they're talking about, either.

It comes down to a plain citizen staying with an issue, understanding it politically, and using common sense. I'm very often reminded of the

Emperor's new clothes. You go to a hearing and it is baloney from beginning to end, with rationale upon rationale for why something should be done and why it would work, when simple, plain common sense will tell you that this is a bad thing to do. They love to say to citizens at public hearings: "Well, Mrs. So-and-so, you certainly condemned that. But we have a traffic problem. What should we do?" If this happens after several hours of explaining what is needed and how it should work, then the answer is, "That is why you are being paid $30,000 a year. You go back to your drawing board and you come up with a plan that we, as citizens, can live with."

II. Housing

Morton Isler (Director of Housing Studies, the Urban Institute): Essentially, my message is that people who are concerned with the urban housing situation are not necessarily in conflict with people who are concerned about conservation. There are, as Chuck Little has pointed out, specific situations where it becomes an either/or situation—either open space or housing. It's a very hard thing to do. When one mentions the word "ecology" (or "conservation" or "housing"), one automatically gets a set of associations. I think when one mentions housing, typically in this country, people will say, "We're going to build something." That's construction. If you've got a housing program, it's a building program, it seems to follow.

Our view, and all of our work, is based on the notion that housing is not a building thing, but a service—a service people get from living in a particular dwelling. So we talk about housing services.

Why do we think about housing as construction or something? Well, basically it's because our public programs in housing evolved in the '30s. I think there were a lot of appropriate reasons for housing to be a construction thing in the '30s, and those reasons have basically disappeared.

First of all, housing programs were developed as employment programs. They were WPA projects, in a sense—a way of getting people into jobs. Secondly, in our cities and in our rural areas in the '30s, we had a lot of substandard housing, dilapidated housing—the famous picture of the shack in the shadow of the Capitol—which you really couldn't do much with to provide satisfactory housing services.

In our cities, those buildings or shacks are gone. They may be gone for the wrong reason, such as putting a highway through. But the fact is that they are really no longer there. The dilapidated housing that we now have in our cities is really a result of the misuse of housing resources, rather than something that is fundamentally structural. The dilapidation of housing is, for the most part, the result of human decisions, rather than structural construction problems.

90

Yet we still have essentially the same housing programs today that we had in the '30s, supported essentially by a group of people bent on constructing things—labor unions, the National Association of Home Builders, etc. We now build about two million housing units a year which, as Secretary [of Housing and Urban Development] Romney is fond of pointing out, is over twice the rate of household growth in this country. The issue is why we build so much housing, and I'll come back to that in a minute.

Accompanied by that, I think many people recognize the tremendous destruction of housing that's going on in our cities, leading very often to the abandonment of large areas of a city, such as Brownsville in New York and Roxbury in Boston, parts of north Philadelphia, and so forth. So, in effect, what the new housing programs are doing, at least partly, is replacing housing that's already there—housing, moreover, that is fundamentally sound. Many architects would say that it is structurally more sound than what we're building.

"The dilapidated housing that we have in our cities is really a result of the misuse of housing resources, rather than something that is fundamentally structural."

In the process of going through this building cycle, we're gobbling up larger amounts of land, which is a conservation issue. We're also using large amounts of timber which, a couple of years ago, in terms of our national forests, became a major issue because of the lumber shortage.

We are also seeing something that is probably even more devastating to the poor—tremendous cost inflations in housing. In places like Washington, it's very clear that the pressures that are being put on land—a limited amount of land—are related to this, and ecological issues—such as extending sewers and providing for community facilities that have to accompany housing—are closely related, too.

As a result, in some areas we're getting higher density housing. This may be a good thing. We're seeing an increase in interesting things, like clustering and planned-unit development, and things of that sort which may or may not preserve the land. I'm not sure, but I think they're really the outgrowth, rather than the design, of a conservation policy.

So what I'm saying is that I think housing is a conservation issue right now, and the issue really is more thinking about conserving our housing stock, conserving the opportunities for people to live in socially useful housing, and getting good housing services out of housing in better locations, rather than 30 or 40 miles outside of the cities.

In terms of not driving up the price of land, I see a very mutually consistent set of issues. The vacancy rate isn't going up simply because the more we build, the more we destroy. We're probably destroying units now at a greater rate than we ever have before. I could draw a frightening picture of a sort of system of almost planned obsolescence, where we just keep building and building and abandoning and abandoning.

Well, what do you do about all of this? The two basic elements to a solution are money and housing management. Money is critically needed in poverty areas for people to be able to afford the basic operating costs, and that money doesn't necessarily have to come from a housing program. That money could be an adequate income-maintenance program. With housing management, I'm not talking about what a housing manager does, or a superintendent, but what has to be done on a day-to-day basis—all the interacting behaviors of people, especially the residents of buildings.

Our definition of management would include, for example, single-family housing, where the homeowners essentially play many of the roles of management. They make important consumer choices, such as whether to fix something themselves or to call the plumber. We see no reason why every consumer shouldn't have these opportunities, no matter what kind of tenure you're living under or where you live. A very important component of this is really the whole notion of occupant responsibility, of controlling negative behaviors that we find in certain parts of our cities.

These are the sorts of problems that we're dealing with. We have to do two important things. One, we have to break the old view of what housing is: that housing is building. We have to begin to think about housing as a service. Secondly, we have to find some sort of public program that can really deal with the human behaviors that are destroying the housing stock and creating much of the issue between conservation and housing.

DISCUSSION

Arthur A. Davis (Vice President, the Conservation Foundation): Let me see if I understand you. What you're saying is that much of the housing stock in the central city is basically adequate. The problem is more social and financial, rather than physical. Instead of building somewhere else, we ought to rehabilitate, in a broad sense, what we've got, not just physical structure, but the whole service structure as well.

Isler: It isn't just a matter of rehabilitation; it's a matter of conservation. We have a lot that doesn't need to be rehabilitated; it needs to be conserved. Very often, when the point is reached that something needs to be rehabilitated, it may be better to tear it down. This isn't a pitch for rehabilitation at all—it's a pitch for conservation of housing resources.

Furthermore, I'm not arguing against all construction programs. What I'm arguing for is construction as needed. Certainly, there are questions revolving around whom we construct for and where and so forth, but the fact is: we have 70 million housing units in this country and we add to them very incrementally somewhere between 1.5 and 2 million units a year.

All the attention is focused on that increment, which is not an unimportant issue. It's just that we need to balance it much more. We're faced

---

"I could draw a frightening picture of a sort of system of almost planned obsolescence, where we just keep building and building and abandoning and abandoning."

---

with a situation where, in the political process, the primary proponent of public programs are producers and not consumers—and not even producers of housing services. It's not the real-estate industry that's involved. It's basically the construction world and the building-materials world. It's a very similar, parallel situation to the highway thing.

Pope: It seems to me, in this country, that housing for low-income people has been dealt with in two ways. One is that they inherit old housing which the middle class has moved from. The second is that the great tenements in the big cities have been used as the housing stock for successive waves of poor immigrants and migrants.

I have the impression that, when new housing has been built for the poor, we haven't been able to maintain the quality of the housing, and it has tended to degenerate very rapidly. Yet the good urban neighborhoods we had for working classes have been all middle class. Is that a fair reading of the record?

Isler: Yes. There are important exceptions, but basically I think that is correct.

Pope: Do you think there are any lessons to be drawn from the exceptions?

Isler: My personal view is that we have to think about it primarily in terms of stimulating the opening up of opportunities for low-income people to move into the existing stock in a way in which the stock isn't going to degenerate. I lived in a suburban county where there was a great deal of movement of low-income people into the older villages of the county—into the older housing stock. It was basically good housing stock. It was smaller than the new housing being built, but outside of that there wasn't that much difference.

But the circumstances were such that it almost became a self-fulfilling prophecy that those houses were going to deteriorate. The economic circumstances and the attitudinal circumstances seemed to dictate it. Either there is no opportunity for people to buy the houses they want, or the houses are owned by investors who have the feeling that the market is shot in this particular area and it doesn't pay to keep investing in the house.

John Hampton (National Tenants Organization): I think you made a clear statement that the problem with housing deterioration is the fault of the people that live there. I'd like to make the point that there are many more significant factors involved in the deterioration of housing than just the fact that the people there are poor and have bad attitudes and opportunities.

Isler: If I gave that impression, thank you for correcting me. What I tried to say is that there is a set of institutional arrangements—I mentioned investors, owners, public-housing managers, etc.—that interact and create a situation where the only sensible attitude is to have a negative attitude. My view is that to deal effectively with this set of circumstances, one has to start with the occupants.

Hampton: Let's go back and define the picture a little more carefully so that we can get beyond the question of attitudes and the fact of deterioration. If you take a bunch of people who happen to be poor and qualify for public housing—who have been systematically denied all the things necessary to get a decent job and make a decent amount of money—those people then represent the most abused and exploited section of the population. You push them into public housing, especially designed for them—especially designed to reinforce the fact that, because you're poor, there must be something wrong with you; to reinforce the fact that if you don't make enough money in this country, there must be something wrong inside you. And so, given that kind of housing and the tremendous density it has, and a housing program not committed to even maintaining the junk they built in the first place, and not committed to giving good maintenance in the second place, it falls down. And the thing to do is blame it on the people who live there.

The same thing holds true for the question of private housing, where the slum lords are going to the banks and mortgage companies. Those houses all carry tremendous mortgages, far greater than you ever hope to pay off, which means that there's no money left over for maintenance after the principal and interest are paid. The guy is milking it for all it's worth. It's a clear rip-off! And then you say the reason the house falls apart is attitudinal.

Isler: I'm not willing to accept that I said that—because I *agree* with you about the basic part of the problem. The feelings engendered by that set of circumstances are certainly there. The question is: how does it get changed and what is the process of changing feelings? All I was saying was that unless those feelings are changed and unless the circumstances which create those feelings are changed, there's no real solution to that problem. I wasn't saying that it was the fault of the occupant.

Hampton: One of the things you talked about, however, was money —there's great amounts of money being made off this construction of subsidized housing. Another important thing you mentioned was the fact that the real beneficiaries of the program are not the consumers or the ultimate people who provide the services through their housing, but the builders and financiers. The same holds true for highways. The same holds true for the big battle over timber, over strip mining. It's not the people who work there or the people who buy there or live there, but the guys that make some money who are calling the shots.

Buie Seawell (Assistant to the Director, Rocky Mountain Center on the Environment): In all of these issues—and housing particularly—it's a basic question of who controls the environment that people live in. Is it the people that live there, or someone else? It is at the community level where housing either makes it or doesn't. And who controls the shape and form of that community, who planned it, how the different units relate to each other, is a key environmental question and also a basic social-

---

"Housing is location. Housing offers a family their basic location in the universe and their opportunities for accessibility to other opportunities in society."

---

justice question. When people control the communities they live in socially and politically, they will have justice for themselves, whether it's on the issue of blocking highways or providing jobs or housing or whatever.

Davis: I agree that this is a fundamental focus we ought to be talking about. But we do want to go through these functional concerns which are all so dreadfully important.

Paul Davidoff (Co-Director, Suburban Action Institute): I just want to propose a sort of alternative perspective toward what Mort just said. I would think that the production of 2.6 million housing units is probably, at most, an adequate standard.

But housing is more than structure or service. Housing is location. Housing offers a family their basic location in the universe and their opportunities for accessibility to other opportunities in society—educational amenities, employment, first of all. At least for some of us today, we see the great necessity of expanding housing opportunity in the suburbs and beyond—because this is where the growth of the nation is taking place.

We see the opportunity for constructing housing of the mixed-income variety to break away from our segregation of low-income housing or upper-income housing, which has been the pattern in the suburbs thus far, as providing a basis for a new type of community and, at the same time, providing us with the room necessary to reconstruct our cities for more livable 21st Century densities.

III. Employment

Wayne Redus (Employment Director, San Francisco Human Rights Commission): What I want to talk about are some of the issues that separate the working stiff from environmental types. I also want to talk about some of the ways to maybe get people together.

One of the things that separates the groups is a kind of superior "I know best" attitude on the part of the environmentalists. I've noticed a real pervasive kind of thing coming out of a lot of people that I see who say that they are environmentalists, and who also say that they "know best." That kind of attitude puts off a lot of people, especially if you're talking about a union member, and causes the kind of paranoia that exists between labor and the environment.

Labor says that environmentalists don't give a damn about jobs, just a bunch of white, middle-class elitists who live in the suburbs and don't care about jobs. Well, that's not really true. There's nobody here that I can imagine who doesn't care about jobs. Everybody here probably feels that people who want to work should be able to work, so if all the BS is taken out, we can get down to the fact that that's one of the common things that people do feel.

On the other hand, environmentalists seem to think that labor doesn't care about the environment. John Yolton helped us to see that that's not necessarily true. One of the things I planned to point out was that most international unions and most of their locals do have some kind of environmental committee. So that kind of consciousness is involved with the "union mind."

That gets into the next thing, which is prejudice about what the union mind is. Often, people who are not involved in the trades union movement look at unions as if unions were filled with a bunch of dums-dums who don't know anything. Senator Newhouse, yesterday, made some really weird statement about how, if you're white and don't have any talent and you're lazy, you can always become a carpenter.

Certainly, in rank-and-file situations, you're going to find people who meet that kind of description. You're going to find that in the military, you're going to find that in an office, and you're going to find that kind of mediocrity anywhere. Unions don't have a monopoly on mediocrity. As a matter of fact, union leadership, because of its constituency, has to look

96

into and represent a range of issues that perhaps other kinds of special interest groups don't have to address. The *Federalist,* a small unionist magazine, must deal very, very specifically and in detail with diverse topics that you just normally wouldn't even read about in most trade papers.

So the union mind—whatever that means—doesn't necessarily mean this guy who maybe wears a hard hat and has a beer belly and goes around beating up on hippies and queers.

I did want to bring out a couple of facts—and I'm reacting about this union thing because I've noticed a real heavy and maybe subtle anti-union, or at least "unions-aren't-people-you-should-work-with" feeling coming out of this group. Senator Newhouse had some problems with the apprenticeship programs. He said that you can't get minorities involved in the construction trades because the unions won't let them in. This hasn't been exactly our experience in San Francisco.

The traditional course to get minorities into trade unionism is through a Philadelphia Plan or a California Plan or whatever. We found those kinds of procedures just don't work. To a large extent, getting minorities into the building trades depends on the conscious building of relationships with the building-trades leadership (labor), contractors (management), and the community. What you have to do is take the president of the building-trades congress, and feed him and drink with him and, all of a sudden, he finds out you're human and you find out that he's human.

In San Francisco, we've worked out a plan to get minorities into the building trades. So far this year, 45 per cent of all new apprentices in San Francisco have been minority people. Management, labor, and the community participate in what is called the Apprenticeship Opportunities Foundation. This Foundation is governed by a Board of Directors, which is made up of representatives of each group. Since San Francisco is a union town (they decide who is going to be Mayor), we have the Mayor's office behind us.

We are able to say to a contractor on a city construction job that he doesn't have enough minority journeymen. If the contractor says he can't get journeymen, we say what about an apprentice. Then he says the union won't give him one. Then we say to the contractor that he has to go to the Apprenticeship Opportunities Foundation, and they'll provide him with whatever it is he wants—and it works.

Now, let's get down to the issue of jobs and the environment. In San Francisco, we have a good example of classic conflict over issues of the environment, housing, transportation, and employment in the proposed Yerba Buena Center. This is a redevelopment plan for a convention, sports, and commercial center. The controversy has been housing and environment against jobs.

When we talk about convention facilities, a lot of people say that that has nothing to do with people in the city. But San Francisco is a weird place, and it happens to be a place that depends, to a large extent, on tourists coming there. But they're not going to come there if they can't find places to meet, if they can't find places to sleep or eat, or if there is no way to get there. So if Yerba Buena can be built and the hotel can be built, there will be some jobs there.

There are a lot of people, however, really concerned that Yerba Buena is going to adversely affect the environment. Sewers have to be relocated; all kinds of things. An environmental impact study for Yerba Buena is going to cost at least $250,000. Now, what I want to know is, who is going to get that $250,000?

I see some environmentalist consulting firm getting that 250 thou. I see that kind of money being sliced off, and see the kind that Joe Doakes is going to make by selling hot dogs at the sports arena being wiped off by this guy getting $250 thousand for that kind of study. Now, I'm not arguing with the concept or the need for an environmental study, but I am saying that it seems awfully weird, when there are people bumming on that street corner for a cup of coffee or a bottle of muscatel, somebody is going to rip off 250 thou to make a study to find out what the environmental impacts are going to be.

So, here is an issue that divides the environmental group and some of the people who need work. And it's not just a racial or minority issue, because a lot of those people who need work are poor whites. There are 25,000 unemployed in San Francisco. Yerba Buena, from construction through operation, will provide at least 12,000 jobs. Now, that's not magically erasing half the unemployment rate in San Francisco, but it's doing a large bit for it.

"Are we really saying that the environmentalists are going to win out or that people who need jobs are going to win out? Do we have to choose sides and go out and fight each other? I don't think we do."

The California Building Trades Council estimated that, since environmental legislation has occurred, $7 billion in construction delays has resulted. I don't know if this is true or not—it's a labor estimate. But the fact is that, with the studies, with the court actions, with all the delays—that's expensive; that's money lost or spent; and it's not going to the people who need work.

98

Lending institutions are starting to really worry about their money. They become very suspect about any kind of construction project that's going to involve the environmental issue, because that means there may be court delays and it may never even get built. There are people walking around San Francisco who believe that Yerba Buena will never happen—that it will just sit there. A lot of people think that BART will just eventually sink into the Bay and not work at all.

Most cities are doing what they can to push the blue-collar people out. They do it by pushing industry out. San Francisco, for example, is involved in a very conscious effort to become the banking, financial, and insurance center of the West, which it already is but somehow doesn't feel secure enough and wants to become even more so. So what you get is a redevelopment policy—a planning policy that encourages high-rise office buildings and discourages industry and middle-class neighborhoods.

". . . the environmental movement has done nothing that's been articulated or individualized to make people who are non-elite, non-white, and non-middle-class welcome in the movement, and that's what I think has to be done."

During the 1960's, San Francisco lost approximately 14,000 blue-collar jobs because of San Francisco's concerted effort to drive blue-collar jobs out of the city. So when the Human Rights Commission goes to an employer and says, why don't you hire some of these blue-collar types, the employer says he is in the process of cutting down on his operation because the city obviously doesn't want him. We find this whenever we talk with industrial people.

Construction and port development must also happen for jobs to happen. Port development is, of course, anti-environmental, if you look at it on the surface; port development meaning, to some extent, land fills, dredging, and piers. It may mean a U.S. Steel building out on a pier. It may mean taking access to the Bay away from the people—all kinds of things.

However, San Francisco and all other port towns have to continue to develop their ports just to exist. The ships the Japanese are making are becoming increasingly huge, and a lot of them are already too big for the major ports to handle. So there's got to be port development.

Are we really saying that the environmentalists are going to win out or that people who need jobs are going to win out? Do we have to choose sides and go out and fight each other? I don't think we do.

Leonard Woodcock, the president of the UAW, talks about a new social ethic, which is kind of corny. However, its basic assumption is that there's a basic right in both environmental *and* economic security, and that that right can be implemented only by setting the priorities in that direction and by providing the means.

What it really comes down to is money. There's the cost factor and the benefit factor, and what we've talked about so far is the cost factor toward the poor people, and the benefit factor toward the rich. There has got to be a more equitable distribution of costs and benefits in terms of both economic and environmental considerations. And that gets back to what we were talking about before—the redistribution of wealth.

Finally, I have some suggestions for getting the environmental movement together. Go to the individual offices of organizations in the environmental movement and look at the staffs and look at the leadership. You don't find many minorities in environmental offices.

This is supposition on my part, based on my own experiences, but there is nothing in the appearance of these organizations to show me—a black man—that I can participate. I know, out of personal experience, that I can, but there is nothing there to show me this. I've never seen one black person, and I've only seen one Asian woman, in the offices of these organizations. That's something we have to deal with. As far as my experience goes, the environmental movement has done nothing that's been articulated or individualized to make people who are non-elite, non-white, and non-middle class welcome in the movement, and that's what I think has to be done.

There should be some kind of effort on the part of environmentalists to get minorities, not only into the wilderness but to continually return to the wilderness. There are all kinds of programs for taking black children into the woods for the day and showing them what a far-out time it is, and they don't know why the kids don't come back. They don't come back 'cause they were taken on a picnic on a Saturday and they were shown a good time, and that was it! Why should they come back to that? They can do that at home.

The campership programs, especially primitive-type backpacking, I think, are very good. They bring counselors—who normally would not counsel in that kind of situation (both minorities and non-minorities)—and they also bring campers who would not fit into it. Some return and some do not. But what I'm saying is: if people begin to feel a sense of themselves invested in something, they're going to appreciate it and want to work for it.

And so, inasmuch as I think employment is a very important issue, especially in the cities and the towns, I also think there's going to have to be a lot done in terms of getting minorities involved in what the hell you're talking about!

DISCUSSION

Pankowski: This thing can cut two ways. Many environmentalists don't feel welcome working on inner-city problems. We're in a position to take folks from the city out into the wilderness, but who is to take us into the inner city? We have a tough time convincing conservationists who live in the suburbs to drive in to a hearing in the inner city, much less get involved on a regular basis, because they're not sure they're going to be welcome.

". . . there is real reason for a minority kid, who grew up with rats or roaches, to be afraid of the country because there are spiders out there!"

Redus: That is a problem. Most people are prevented from getting into it out of fear, and sometimes there is a lot of reason for that fear, just as there is real reason for a minority kid, who grew up with rats or roaches, to be afraid of the country because there are spiders out there!

Pope: The big question in all of our cities is: "Whose cities are they going to be?" I think it's probably impossible to maintain long-range effective alliances with cities which are exclusively dominated by minorities. I think there are a lot of people in Washington, say, who feel sufficiently insecure about living with whites for various different historical reasons. They would probably rather see us all leave. Then it would be clear whose turf it was.

But I suspect that creates all kinds of problems for working alliances.

Lawrence Burr (General Manager, State Park Commission for the City of New York): I think the matter of achieving balance, not just in terms of the urban scene but the inner-city scene, is not so much a problem of a population balance distribution as it is a restructuring of power. This is at the heart of the whole thing. Now I don't give a damn if you're white, black, or green, when you talk about the historical process, the problem is that the poor—from the inception, almost, of this country—have been read out of the picture. Today, there is just no inclusion—right now, we're really gassing when we talk about the inner-city people being included and being involved.

Hell, no, we don't want no involvement. This is one of the stark naked truths that this country has got to come to terms with. We're deceiving ourselves if we even talk about the kind of involvement that produces the thing that you're alluding to. I think we're wasting time, sitting around talking about this kind of nonsense—because we're not committed to it.

101

We've got to restructure power in this country. People who happen to live in inner cities are going to have to be involved in every facet of planning, in every facet of living. The whole job thing has got to be restructured. Job training? To hell with job training! It's a waste of time. It does not lead to relevant, ongoing jobs.

I just don't think we're even beginning to deal with facts and realities yet. The inner city is only symptomatic of what I think is a national pastime.

Isler: I think that's an important thing. My view increasingly is that you don't do that by talking generalities. You do it by talking about how do you restructure employment systems. How do you restructure the housing system so that you retransfer power? How do you deal with the whole problem, in the area of conservation and environment, of who has the power to raise the issues and so forth?

CHAPTER VII

Dialogue: Controlling Economic Growth

I. *Sam Love, Coordinator*
Environmental Action, Inc.
Washington, D. C.

II. *Keith Roberts, Attorney-at-Law*
McCray and Roberts
San Francisco, California

III. *Professor Charles Cicchetti*
Department of Economics
University of Wisconsin
Madison, Wisconsin

I

Sam Love: I've put some notes together, really some thoughts that are going through my mind, that I think are relevant to understanding where we are today. I've titled it "The Growing Movement toward Non-Growth," which indicates the type of contradiction we're all trying to resolve.

I feel that we are at an historical moment. There are changes occurring in society which one day will be seen to be as dramatic as the change that occurred with the shift from hunting and gathering to agriculture, or the shift from agriculture to industry. I think what's happening is that a new system of logic is beginning to undergird society. A new socio-economic theory is evolving. None of us have all of the theses to articulate what this new theory will be, but I believe they are evolving. Certainly, within our lifetime, I feel that we'll see it.

There are only a few moments in economic history comparable to this. One is probably the period in which Adam Smith functioned. The predominant economic theory of the day was mercantilism, which basically said that economic activity should be bent toward the political end of national power.

103

But what began to happen was that a subversive group of people began to emerge—the burghers, who were, in a real sense, the first capitalists. What happened was that market systems began to evolve, different forms of exchange began to develop, and it didn't all fit into the mercantilism theory. The mercantilists were having trouble resolving all of it. So Adam Smith wrote a book called *The Wealth of Nations*. This one work really did not invent a new economy. The new economy was already functioning in the society. All he did was describe the new reality. And, in time, that new interpretation of reality shattered an entire economic theory.

"I believe that the debate over equilibrium, over non-growth economics, is the debate that's going to give us the blueprint for the new system."

The transformation to capitalism took hundreds of years, and Adam Smith's work was only the high-water mark. In its early days, capitalism was a very radical economic theory and inherently subversive.

The next historical turning point is Karl Marx's work. In *Das Kapital*, he described two sources of wealth: labor and land—the social and the natural. When he talked about land, he really meant resources. He said that the capitalist, in his unrestrained pursuit of profit, would abuse both the social and the natural.

So, in a sense, that is what we are dealing with now—the abuse of both the social and the natural. In the 1972 Congressional race, Congressman Ken Hechler, running for reelection from West Virginia, put this very well. The major issue facing him was strip mining, and he had become a major proponent for a ban on strip mining. Hechler said, "I told them I was against the exploitation of land because it was also the exploitation of people." In a sense, he is only paraphrasing what Marx said a long, long time ago.

Marx's work, of course, goes on to critique the social abuses. He really didn't deal with the natural abuses. So the socialist movement that emerged out of his theory is almost a one-dimensional movement. It needs another dimension added to it before it can really be complete.

Until recently, we have given little consideration to systems. But finally, out of pure necessity, we are beginning. We are seeing that there are limits to the ecological system and that we are pushing them very close in some areas. There are major political problems evolving because of resource utilization. A recent study by the Chase Manhattan Bank says that, in 1985, the (trade) deficit from the importation of oil and gas to the U.S.

will be $35 billion per year because of our voracious consumption patterns in this country.

To alleviate the crunch, we're trying to work out a deal with the Russians for natural gas in exchange for soy beans. In addition, we've got Arab sheiks with their fingers on the oil faucet, creating a situation that is very politically volatile. All because we can't deal with the natural abuses and the spiraling growth rates in our society. We've also broken nature's circle, as Barry Commoner has so beautifully shown in his book, *The Closing Circle*.

I believe that, in many instances, the system that Adam Smith articulated in the 1750s is reaching its historical limits and that the foundation is being laid for new socio-economic systems. I don't have all the blueprints of what that new system is going to look like, but I believe that the debate over equilibrium, over non-growth economics, is the debate that's going to give us the blueprint for the new system.

I've attempted to look for guidance in some of the classical economists, and I found that John Stuart Mill, in 1848, probably had something to say to us. In the book, *Principles of Political Economy*, he had a chapter on the "stationary state," and there are a couple of paragraphs I'd like to read to you.

> Most fitting, indeed, is it that while riches are power, and to grow as rich as possible the universal object of ambition, the path to its attainment should be open to all, without favour or partiality. But the best state for human nature is that in which, while no one is poor, no one desires to be richer, nor has any reason to fear being thrust back, by the efforts of others to push themselves forward.

And he goes on to say:

> It is scarcely necessary to remark that a stationary condition of capital and population implies no stationary state of human improvement. There would be as much scope as ever for all kinds of mental culture, and moral and social progress; as much room for improving the Art of Living, and much more likelihood of its being improved, when minds cease to be engrossed by the art of getting on.

Herman Daly, an economist who is doing quite a bit of writing on equilibrium economics now, came up with what could be a classical phrase when he said that the politicians who refuse to deal with the inequities of today's society—by putting off dealing with those inequities until tomorrow, on the basis that things are going to get better through continued growth— are nothing more than latter-day Marie Antoinettes, saying "Let them eat growth."

That's where we are, I think. The political structure is not willing to deal with the real problem. It's saying, instead, "Let them eat growth." What we've got to do is deal with the problem now, and we've got to cut

105

through (for the lack of a better term) all this incredible BS that's surrounding us.

I'm not going to pretend that socialism is the answer, because I think that what we must do is so radical that it will even shake up the socialists and communists. But I do think the answers are emerging, and we can't be afraid to embrace them.

There are two ways we can get to an equilibrium state. One is to freeze the relationships that exist now. We could freeze the relationship which has one per cent of the population owning about 75 per cent of the stock in the corporations—the wealth-producing mechanism. We could freeze that. That would be like one group climbing up on top, and then pulling the ladder up behind so that the group down at the bottom could never start to climb up. That's one way to deal with it. We could reach equilibrium like that, and the haves could keep what they have, and the have-nots could keep what they have not, and presumably everybody would be happy.

But it's not likely that everybody would be happy. So there is another way to deal with it. Mills also offers some guidelines in this situation. What he says is that to achieve an equilibrium economy—and he calls it a stationary-state economy—what we really have to do is control population growth and redistribute the wealth. For redistribution of wealth, the mechanism he offers is that people be allowed to keep what is earned with the "final fruits" of their economy, but that there should be a limitation of the sum which any one person may acquire by gift or inheritance to an

---

". . . redistribution can be a unifying force for our movement."

---

amount sufficient to constitute a moderate independence. He would essentially use the plan that McGovern suggested in California—a limitation of $500,000 on inheritance. That would redistribute some wealth, and begin the move toward a stationary state.

Now, there are some problems with this. I don't think that this is all the answer we need. Certainly, the technological changes that Commoner talks about in *The Closing Circle* have to be dealt with. Also, part of the problem is that we have a political system which operates on the theory of domination by quantity. Anybody who's got 51 per cent can try to rule. If you're 12 per cent of the population, you're never going to be too excited about this particular political concept. Certainly, the concerns of the minority communities about population control, which would prevent them from becoming 51 per cent, have some validity.

What emerges out of all this is the fact that redistribution can be a unifying force for our movement. There are clear ecological reasons why we have to move in that direction. There are clear social reasons why we should move in that direction.

How is this redistribution going to come about? I think that we have to begin the debate within our own organizations. It may take the form of attempting to get a resolution through the Sierra Club and having people fight each other on the floor. It may take the form of a type of graduated income tax proposal that some states voted on recently, or equalization of property taxes. In some cases, we can even attempt to pull off structural changes in the economic institutions around us. For example, if we can move private utilities from being private utilities to being public utilities of a nonprofit nature, that can begin to affect redistribution.

II

Keith Roberts (environmentalist and attorney, San Francisco): The first thing I want to talk about is this term "growth." A lot of people have very easily slid into the rhetoric of saying growth is bad and must be limited.

I have here a newspaper article about an association known as the Association of Bay Area Governments, and the headline reads, "ABAG Votes to Limit Bay Growth." This starts out: "In a major victory for the burgeoning environmental cause, ABAG voted 41-10 that official agencies should plan for a population of no more than 5½ million people by 1980." It then goes on to list the actions they call for.

The actions called for are the following: "To establish land-use control to set a limit on planned residential areas; to restrict accessibility and urban services, such as transportation and water and sewer systems; to limit locations and types of industries through zoning policies; to create tax penalties on economic developments that are responsible for the biggest population increase; to set stringent pollution control policies that curtail growth; and to reform local tax structures so communities are not forced to rely so much on growth-oriented property taxes for revenue."

Now, I'd be prepared to argue with any of you that every single one of the measures proposed is calculated to do either precisely the opposite of what they say they're supposed to do, or to wreak havoc, chaos, and unnecessary problems on the Bay area. If there's any one theme I wish to talk about today it's that too often we environmentalists go out and don't know how to go about getting what we're asking for. We ask for the wrong things, and we don't understand how the system works. And so we try a zoning approach or we attack the property taxes or try to limit them without realizing that, by these very measures, we very often create worse environmental problems than we had to begin with.

What do environmentalists mean when they talk about limiting growth? I think that they're talking about limiting certain types of growth. If you're talking about putting a ceiling on the economic system in some arbitrary way, then I think you're talking nonsense, you're talking through your hat, and you're talking in very dangerous rhetoric which is too easily used against us.

It's an example of the rather shallow thinking that sometimes creeps into the environmental movement. The book *The Limits to Growth,* which

---

"If you're talking about putting a ceiling on the economic system in some arbitrary way, then I think you're talking nonsense . . . it's very dangerous rhetoric which is too easily used against us."

---

has stimulated a lot of the thinking here, is another. I think this book has been very severely criticized by a lot of people, and I don't want to go over the criticisms. But, again, it illustrates some of the problems for the environmental movement that have to be attacked—and preferably from within, at this point.

The first one is that it demonstrates, in the data it uses and the manipulations that it performs on those data in order to reach its conclusions—at least in the fields that I'm familiar with (agriculture, economics, etc.)— essentially a complete misunderstanding of what agriculture is about. In other words, this is a guy who is a genius at computer programming and who has decided he's going to take his field and apply it to the whole world, and he doesn't take the care in extending his theory that he did in building his reputation. That's the first type of problem with that book.

The second type of problem with the book is the one that a lot of people have been talking about here. In saying that we must limit growth because it is growth which is causing our misery and our problems, it's ignoring an alternate theory which people have been advancing for quite a long time and which, I think, has a great deal more support in the evidence. This is the theory that it is the distribution of wealth and the distribution of power (which is the same thing, more or less) which is much more at fault in our system. To say "let's limit growth because we can't change the distribution of wealth and power" is a very despairing sort of counsel indeed.

Let me move, then, from these criticisms of the general theoretical concepts, which seem to be becoming more popular in the environmental movement in terms of growth, to the types of panaceas that environmentalists have occasionally proposed. I'd like to talk about three of them.

108

The first of them is the concept of planning. Planners will say, "If only we had the right control of land use, then everything would be okay. If only we had the right system of zoning, . . . " etc. But what it comes down to is that planning is something that the rich can do and the poor can't do.

In the Bay area, it means that poorer cities, like Hayward, can't afford controls. They need all the industry they can get, while in the richer areas, like Mill Valley, you can put on even the most unreasonable kinds of controls and keep out all development—all in the name of good environment.

"To say, 'Let's limit growth because we can't change the distribution of wealth and power' is a very despairing sort of counsel."

Sometimes it's motivated by racism, sometimes it's just misguided. To the poor or to the small shopkeeper, for example, planning works as a totally arbitrary system. Of course, there are administrative appeals; there are ways of bribing people, maybe. But usually the small shopkeeper doesn't have the money to pursue it. If he's turned down by the zoning board, that's it.

In my town of Berkeley, you can't open a barber shop without getting a permit from someone or other. If that guy doesn't like your face, he can turn you down. He can break the law and you have no recourse because you don't have the money to do anything about it. Whereas, if I were to come to Berkeley with a $90-million development tomorrow, I could probably get a variance.

So what happens is that zoning means environmental protection against the poor, and no environmental protection against the rich. If you try to impose planning concepts on top of an economic system which is paying people to violate those concepts, you're not going to be very successful unless you're in a very rich community which can afford to stick to its guns.

There's a second kind of panacea which some environmentalists have embraced, which is a sort of throw-back to the New Deal psychosis of creating more agencies. Let's have an agency to protect this and an agency to protect that. I'd like to read a comment about that approach, which was written in 1793 by a guy named William Godwin, who was a political philosopher. He pointed out, talking about legislation:

> First, then, legislation is, in almost every country, grossly the favour of the rich against the poor. Such is the character of the game laws, by which the industrious rustic is forbidden to destroy the animal that preys upon the hopes of his future subsistence or to supply himself with the food that, unsought, thrusts itself in his path. Such was the

109

spirit of the late revenue laws of France which, in several of their provisions, fell exclusively upon the humble and industrious, and exempted from their operations those who were best able to support them. Thus, in England, the land tax at this moment produces half a million less than it did a century ago, while the taxes on consumption have experienced an addition of 13 millions per annum during the same period. This is an attempt, whether effectual or no, to throw the burden from the rich upon the poor and, as such, is an example of the spirit of legislation.

Government, right now, is primarily an instrument of benefit to the powers that be. If that's not true of an agency in its initial creation, in a few years it will be. We should be very suspicious of this "more-government-will-solve-the-problems" panacea.

Now, there's a third panacea, of which a lot has been heard at this gathering—the simplistic call to redistribute the wealth. If we redistributed all the wealth in this country tomorrow, in 25 years we'd have the same sys-

---

"If we redistributed all the wealth in this country tomorrow, in 25 years we'd have the same system again."

---

tem again. I won't get into a discussion of the rhetoric of the environmental movement, but proclaiming yourself radical, or innovative, or against the free-enterprise system is not, in my opinion, a very sure path to success at this point.

There is good news, though! There are two positive things to say.

One is that the government is basically responsible for the kinds of problems we're talking about. Secondly, there remains the possibility of our gaining control of the government. Most environmental abuses are either caused by the government, subsidized by the government, or carried out in violation of existing laws which the government has already passed. So we can look to the government and change the governmental policies to have a significant environmental effect.

A couple of generalizations can be drawn out of what I've been telling you. One is that it is both simple and unhealthful to say that environmental improvement costs fall hardest on the poor and the middle class. They do if you use the present tax system. But it can be arranged so that they don't, and it's obvious that this should be done.

I also think that it's unhealthful for us to wait for some fundamental redistribution of wealth before we do something about these environmental problems, because that takes a long time. Besides, the problem isn't really

110

economic. It's legal and political—because who pays has always been the primary political question in this country. The law limits what kind of answer we can give. In this case, the legal question that we really face, and the one I think we should address, is, "Who owns the environment?"

If corporations own the environment—to do what they want—then we must buy it back from them. We must pay them for pollution control. We must pay them their price, whatever they can exact from us for what we want. If we, the public, own the environment, however, we can then turn around and force the corporations to pay us for that environment. I think it's that conceptual problem we ought to face—the question of who owns it.

III

Charles Cicchetti (professor of economics, University of Wisconsin): I'm going to talk about three categories today, two of which I thought about before I came, and the third since I've been here. But before I do, the first issue I should address is the one Keith (Roberts) raised—"Who owns the environment?" Not making that decision, in fact, says that it's owned by all, and all can do whatever they want with it. That means that firms will just continue to pollute.

Let's first talk about the economic effects of pollution control. Pollution controls, whatever they are and whatever form they take, are always going to be met by hostile reactions from the chambers of commerce, from national and local associations of manufacturers who claim that pollution control is going to cost a loss of jobs, higher prices, firms closing down and moving away, and just a massive disruption to the economic activity. My position and that of others who have studied the eleven most polluting industries is that this is a bit of an overstatement.

Let's take them in order. First, plant closings. The conclusion of studies that looked at plant closings was that no firm that would have continued operation for the next ten years would be forced to close by any of the pollution-control measures that are currently on the books. Some of those that might have closed in ten years may close in five years if pollution controls were put in. So it's a speed-up in plant closings, but not any actual change in plant closings until the next decade.

What about jobs? To answer the question on jobs, you have to say what is the effect of pollution control going to be on prices. Prices will probably be affected no more than 10 per cent, if that. This means that the overall effect of pollution controls on consumption—that is, the amount of goods that a particular industry might have to produce—is going to be relatively small.

So, if plants close or plants change because of pollution-control measures, you're going to have to hire labor and hire workers to work in other plants which might be less polluting. There will be a displacement of jobs.

111

Some workers will be forced to move from one place to another, but there shouldn't be any measurable or appreciable drop in jobs as a result of pollution-control costs than are presently being forced on industry.

There's even a more subtle connection between jobs and pollution control. That is, that as long as the environment and using the environment

---

"The net effect is: if you start to put a price tag on the environment, this changes the direction of economic activity — but it should change in the direction of more jobs, rather than less jobs."

---

is free, industry will continue to use as much of the environment as an input to production as it can. Once it has to pay for using the environment, it's going to use less environment to produce its goods and services, and that means it's going to use more of other inputs for production. It means that if the environment is no longer free, firms are going to have to invest in equipment to control pollution, invest in labor to deal with solid-waste and pollution-control problems, and new jobs will be opening up in the industries that produce such equipment.

So the net effect is: if you start to put a price tag on the environment, this changes the direction of economic activity, but it should change in the direction of more jobs, rather than less jobs.

Now, I'd like to turn to the issue of growth-no growth—the Club of Rome thesis versus Keynesian economics, or whatever. I have sort of a simplistic view of the extreme positions that are represented by so-called Keynesian economics and the so-called Club of Rome. I tend to split people into these two groups, although I don't think anyone is really in either of these extreme positions.

I describe these two groups or positions in the context of two syndromes. The first I call the *Apollo syndrome*—the "if-we-can-put-a-man-on-the-moon-we-can-do-anything" syndrome. In these lights, all environmental problems, no matter how complex, are soluble. On the opposite side, I see the *Vietnam syndrome*. It goes like this: "If we can't get out of Vietnam, how can we do anything as a society?" Therefore, the environmental problem is just something else that we can't do anything about. We've just got to sit back and hopefully put off the day of reckoning.

I don't believe that either of these syndromes is very accurate. I tend to think of the so-called Keynesian growth position as the Apollo syndrome —that technology is going to change, that relative prices will reflect the changing costs that pollution is generating, that people will adjust to pollution by initiating technical change which will solve all our problems.

112

My mind foresees a kind of massive plumbing system, with every waste recycling around it.

On the other hand, the Vietnam syndrome of no-growth—that there's nothing we can do, there's no positive advancement that can take place—

"The growth nexus we're in, with an ever-expanding GNP, hasn't really solved any of the distribution problems either."

---

is equally simplistic. I think that if there's a main point—and a point to this conference—that has to be and should be addressed, it's the distributional effects of either extreme for anything in the middle. We've heard people say that the Club of Rome should be criticized, or the no-growth position should be criticized because of the distributional implications of no-growth. That is, no-growth means that the pie is not going to get any bigger and unless we address the distribution problem, the haves will keep what they have and the have-nots will have not.

On the other hand, the growth nexus that we're in, with an ever-expanding GNP, hasn't really solved any of the distribution problems either. I don't think either extreme, either the continuation-of-growth solution or the no-growth solution, necessarily solves the distribution problem.

There's another issue I'd like to raise. The preceding speaker talked about redistribution in this country. What about redistribution around the world? If you think about redistribution and if you think about no-growth, it's probably not enough to think of redistribution in this country as the only objective. Aren't the closing circle or the economic and environmental dilemmas that we're facing world dilemmas, not national dilemmas?

Finally, I want to get to the thing that I find most interesting. That is, an examination of the institutions which exist in this country and the way they impact the problems of both the environment and the social community. Institutions in this country encourage several things. They encourage growth. They encourage energy use. They encourage the accumulation of wealth, and they respond most accurately to power and to wealth, making the distribution of income tend toward inequity.

It seems to me that many of the institutions we have are examples of situations of where the rich are getting richer, the environment is being more damaged, and the very existence of these institutions is where we have to begin to look to address our problems. It's too simple to say, "I'm against economic growth" or "I'm against a rising GNP, and I'm for a cleaner environment and I'm for social justice, and I'm going to vote liberally." What we really have to do is go in and find out about our institutional policies and find out how they affect distribution. The way I've sustained my interest in environmental policies is that most times, when I scratch an environmental question, I've found a greedy capitalist or a greedy individual who was getting the rip-offs and who was getting Congress or government agencies or somebody to help him find a way of beating the system and making his position better, relative to the rest of his competitors and, at the same time, destroying the environment.

Let me give you some examples. We've all heard of the Alaska pipeline. Ultimately, the Alaska pipeline is supposed to bring two million barrels of oil per day to help solve the energy crisis in this country. But the more we dug around the pipeline issue, the more we found. California wasn't the place where the oil was going to be marketed, as the oil companies had said. In fact, the oil was going to be sold to Japan or brought around through a pipeline in Central America to be refined in the Virgin Islands.

Both of these plans would involve beating the present mandatory oil import quota problem and beating the present restrictions on shipping (called the Jones Act). Those are the things that most economists and most social activists probably, if they thought about it very long, would condemn. That's not the issue. The issue is that the decision to go ahead and build the Alaska pipeline the way it was going to be built—across the earthquake area and forcing through the settlement of native land claims—was done in such a way that the environment wasn't the consideration. Benefits and cost to this nation weren't the consideration. The real consideration was not how can we make $1 a barrel profit, but how can we make $2 a barrel profit.

There are other environmental issues. We've heard a lot about recycling. What are the probabilities for recycling in this country? Take the example of the aluminum can. In this country, as opposed to western Europe, aluminum cans are almost always produced with virgin bauxite, rather than recycled aluminum. There are a couple of reasons why. One, we have the Interstate Commerce Commission, which says that virgin materials can be transported at lower rates than recycled materials. Secondly, we have electric utilities which say that the more electricity you use, the less you pay. Thus, it becomes cheaper for the industry to refine new materials than to recycle old cans.

Neither of these things is true in western Europe, and the mix of recycled versus virgin aluminum cans is exactly the opposite from this country. Institutions which allow electric utilities to charge lower rates for the more electricity used and the ICC—which says that recycled materials have to be penalized—certainly determine the direction of growth and the way that society goes about providing aluminum cans.

There's also the issue of federal water-resource projects and federal matching funds which encourage localities or municipalities to develop in ways that maximize the share of federal funds they can get, rather than in ways that maximize benefits to the public. The Highway Trust Fund is a great example of that. One of the issues that certainly determines highway construction is the fact that 90 percent of the funds for interstates comes from the federal government. When you get 90 cents on a dollar paid by someone else, and then get all the local benefits which go into the property tax base, maximizing state and local taxes—all these things are very real kinds of institutional incentives.

Defense programs and the political "pork barrel" are another example of how the institutional arrangement has a distributional effect on public expenditure.

The final thing I want to mention is something that Keith Roberts brought up—the Land and Water Conservation Fund. The money is derived from special taxes and revenues, and is to be used for acquisition of land and development of public recreational areas. It is managed by the Bureau of Outdoor Recreation, which decides where the money should go on the basis, presumably, of greatest need. Need is defined by BOR as that area which has the greatest unmet demand. What does that mean? Let's think in their terms to get the kind of philosophy that goes on.

The estimate is made for different income levels, and sometimes even for different races, of what the participation would be in outdoor recreation in a given region. Let's say the average for the region was 20 days for high income and 10 days for low income, and let's say that in a particularly high income area there wasn't any park, and in a particularly low income area, there wasn't any park.

The decision would then be made that we could maximize the amount of benefit from spending this federal Land and Water Conservation Fund money by putting it in the area where there was the greatest unmet demand. Since the high-income area, on the average of the region, would use it 20 days and the low-income area would use it 10 days, it then followed that the high-income area, quite naturally, would get the park. And since they use these statistical determinations every five years, of course the next time they gathered data, the high-income area would have been brought up to its 20, and so the average would move out. So, again, the need would be continuing to grow in the high-income area because now the average across all high-income areas might be 25. So, again, the new parks and the new money would go into the high-income areas.

Certainly, this was the policy and the strategy that was taken.

DISCUSSION

Rev. Scott Paradise (Director, Boston Industrial Mission): Keith, I was interested in what you said, and I join you in pleading for rational, cautious, careful thought about all these questions. Yet I am a little flabbergasted at the kind of attack you level on those who have questions about the viability of growth. I think you've gone to California and come back believing that the world is flat.

I have thought that it was one of the basic principles of ecology that no organism, not even man, can endlessly multiply and exploit a limited environment. You cannot satisfy infinite wants with finite resources. In our pursuit of continued material growth, we are facing environmental limits which are bringing the cause of justice and the cause of a good environment into a collision course.

And I'm surprised, too, when you say you don't know what is meant by growth. Certainly, one thing it means is material growth—growth in the consumption of material resources, growth in population, growth in the use of energy.

Roberts: Scott, let me respond. Obviously, we are against the growth and use of certain kinds of resources in certain ways. But the word "growth" is too simple. We're against mining additional quantities of coal, perhaps, by strip-mining methods. We're against using additional amounts of iron by open pit mining. But that doesn't mean that we're against certain types of growth in economic activity.

I think the use of the word "growth" is just such an overall cap, such a broad term, that to speak of it is very frightening. That's what my criticism was.

Paradise: Well, it's a shorthand, and I would like to have some economist describe to me the possibilities of distinguishing economic growth of non-material things from economic growth which is involved with industry and the production and distribution of material growth.

I think that material growth, generally, if it continues beyond a certain point, can be destructive of the environment. We have seen it erode social health in the human community. In this period of growth, the social health of this country has hardly improved.

It also seems that material growth does not eliminate, or even much reduce, the injustices in society. One might even argue, taking certain things into account, that there's been a widening gap between the rich and the poor, and that growth offers an illusory hope. It doesn't really produce for the poor the way it promises.

This may be because the system is designed to accumulate wealth for those that have it by exploiting the environment and the poor. I was thinking that our ideology of material growth serves the function to keep the poor quiet, to keep them accepting the present state of injustice, and is comparable to the visions of heaven and hell in the Middle Ages.

But this isn't the real issue. I don't know of anyone who is proposing that we stop material growth tomorrow. To slow down growth in the present system—in the present economic, social, and political arrangements —clearly would be to court disaster.

116

The issue is whether it is necessary or whether it's possible to plan a comprehensive, long-range transition—maybe taking 50 years—between the present economic and social system, which depends on material growth for its health, into a system that would somehow achieve a balance between man and the resources of the earth.

If this is the real issue, the important question, then, is how to begin the planning process and the educational process, how to develop a strategy to move in this direction. One of the things I'd like to try to have us do very much while we're together is to begin thinking about the way to move beyond this sort of laundry list of different issues, strung one on top of the other, that we might have a common interest in. See if we can arrive at some overall set of goals or strategies or priorities about how to advance.

Borrelli: One aspect of this growth issue discussion that bothers me is the apparent lack of vision it implies. Where is the vision? I don't think we need plans for the future so much as we need some vision of the future—something like Mills's stationary-state economy. I get a little wary when environmentalists, who have perhaps graduated to the second level of consciousness with regard to the growth issue, begin talking about an economy or a society in which people will not be out ripping off the resources of the world, but will be involving themselves in the educational and cultural and social upliftments of society.

This is all fine, but what about the impact of the transitional period on some people? It's one thing for us to talk about changing a transportation system, for example, and saying how those fellows out there on the UAW assembly line could just as easily be making mass-transit vehicles. But what happens to them in the transition period?

Or how about plant closings? We can say, with some degree of confidence, that those plans would have gone out of business anyway. They've only gone out of business five years earlier. But what do those people do for those five years? Their timetable has been put in some sort of time machine and the circumstances of the environmental movement have caught up with them faster, perhaps, than they were prepared to deal with it.

Going beyond just the transitional issue, there is the issue of what will people do when we have a so-called "steady-state" economy, and one of the major outputs of the society is better education and cultural uplift. I don't deny that that's possible, but I don't feel that we, as environmentalists, at this point, have much vision about how the future is really going to look if our game plan is adopted.

In deference to those in the movement who talk about such things as redistribution of wealth and income in the country, I still think we have to ask ourselves, "What is it at the end of the road?" Is there some light at the end of the road that we can see and define in concrete terms for the mass of people who, perhaps, don't know what we're all about or what our long-range objectives are?

Redus: Let me make a couple of comments in regard to Cicchetti's statement on plant closings and industry relocation, and the statement that it will not mean a net loss of jobs. There are some big hitches to this. One comes in relocation. Who's going to pay for that relocation? If it's someone who's connected to a company town and they don't have the money to go to the big city where there's a job alternative, how are they going to pack up and leave to go where the new factory is?

Another hitch is the whole question of union jurisdiction. Sometimes it's a simple matter of changing locals. Sometimes it's the whole matter of changing the whole union structure. How is one group of machinists going to put up with these auto workers showing up over here and saying, "We're ready to go to work, boys!"

Borrelli: Exactly! And this goes back to the point that Keith made earlier. We environmentalists, who are in a position of effecting a great many of the institutional changes with respect to the environment, have to think out all the ramifications and consequences of our actions. And some of those actions may not be thoroughly desirable in terms of the social justice issues that we're talking about.

Yolton: The whole thing that's wrong is that we never plan for people. Sure, we've got studies going on in environmental dislocation, but we're not coming up with any positive plan—national economic, democratic planning in the country to meet the needs.

It doesn't make any difference in this country, over the years, what our economic growth has been. We've never had enough jobs for people, we've never taken care of living standards for people. We don't have any kind of social planning that relates to people's needs.

Borrelli: You've hit the nail right on the head. What we are involved in, in a great deal of environmental reform, is a form of social planning. That's why I say we need the vision. Though it may sound lofty, we have to know what that social plan is.

Hampton: One of the things, I think, that relates to both the question of economic growth and resource consumption has to do with the allocation of resources to different areas of production. I have read that since World War II—certainly since Korea—95 per cent of the American government-financed research has been war-oriented. Some 57 per cent of all corporations, in one way or another, have a war-related product. That means that the country, and certainly the GNP, to a large extent, is related to war, producing things which have no commodity value and no benefit for people. You can't consume them except in warfare.

Therefore, there is room to discuss the reduction of, let's say, energy requirements. If, indeed, much of the public energy being consumed is being consumed in areas that do not benefit people, you could then talk about reducing the need for that energy while, on the other hand, reducing the output of bombs, tanks, planes, and guns.

118

By the same token, much of the energy of society—in terms of human energy—is directed toward the manufacture of those things. If you're going to reduce the need to build planes, tanks, and guns, you can talk about a reorientation of the goals that go with them toward something that has some human benefit.

Roberts: I agree with what you say, and think that one of the most important programs environmentalists should be behind is one of conversion from a war economy to peace. My personal feeling about politicians right now is that any politician who declares that he's against war or that he's in favor of the environment, and who is not, at the same time, seriously working in favor of conversion planning, is a fraud.

Howe: There's one point that has been touched by indirection, but I am surprised it has not been a major topic this afternoon—the question of incorporating the cost of maintaining environmental quality in the production of goods. The fact that these costs are incorporated in the sale price of those goods still seems not to rest very happily with some social forces. Charles Cicchetti has given us a general factor of 10 per cent as the area of expected cost increase. But even a 10 per cent increase in what people are accustomed to paying for things, because of including environmental controls into the production process, seems to me will go down with some sourness, particularly in some of the social quarters that are represented here.

There has even been some advertising by Mobil Oil Company that suggests that environmentalists are people who are increasing the scarcity and cost of petroleum products. It seems to me that this is a ground on which major industry may seek to divide the kinds of efforts that might begin to coalesce out of our kind of discussion here. I think we need to be quite alert to it.

Cicchetti: The short-run effect of a tax on the environment, or a charge for the use of the environment, certainly is going to make products more expensive because firms won't be able to change their processes and their techniques. But the long-run effect doesn't necessarily follow. In the long run—that is, in a period of ten or fifteen years (not a Keynesian long run, when everyone is dead)—prices of products no longer have to be higher. In fact, they could even turn out to be lower because firms will be altering their operations to correspond to the fact that they now have to pay to use the environment. That's an important point to make.

The other important point to make is that even if consumers of industries which pay taxes or pay costs to clean up have to pay higher prices, that's one of the advantages of putting a tax or charge on the environment because you do want to have people change from the consumption of goods which are produced in a polluting process, to goods which are produced in a non-polluting process.

That's one of the reasons that you want to internalize these kinds of costs of pollution.

Howe: I would agree that, in the long run, life is going to be cheaper and probably nicer when we respect our environment. But, it seems to me, you are saying, yes, in the short run, we do face some increases of on-the-shelf products. And, yet, people like Mobil are trying to divide social and environmental forces on those grounds, and it's very serious.

Roberts: Assuming that's true, if I were leading a black group, I would probably go to the Sierra Club and say something like, "We're going to fight that because we have as much moral clout in Congress as you, and

---

"If we're going to be serious, as some of us are, about achieving an equality of opportunity in society, or an equity, then I think we have to recognize that to do it in a stage of non-growth is going to be impossible in our political situation, except perhaps by some revolutionary means."

---

we come wrapped in as much virtue as you, and we can help the polluters win this one. However, if you're willing to support giving money directly to people for housing, and put an end to 236 housing programs or whatever else, we'll deal." So I think that's the way it should come out.

Cicchetti: There's another point there. Another place that people can agree is in taking on the enemy that's trying to divide. That is, sure, gasoline will cost more if there's a lead tax. But gas is already costing about twice as much as it should because of the oil depletion allowance, production allocations, and import quotas.

This is what I meant about changing the institutional constraints. If we take all these things as givens, there are bound to be points of conflict. I guess what I want to do is start going back and revamping some of the givens as well, because they're mutually defeating to both low-income groups and consumers, in a broader sense, and to environmental interests.

If you can change those things, you can change the direction of society. That, to me, is a more favorable world. That is, change the things that are wrong in society, rather than try to say that you can draw a plan for society and, in our infinite wisdom, tell people what direction they should be going. I certainly don't know how to plan that way and I don't want anyone else to plan that way for me.

Davidoff: As a planner, I am interested in your comments about not wanting someone's image of society imposed on you. I think planning has a very important function. It's not one of imposition, but clearly we need some visions to work with. There's nothing wrong in thinking about visions

120

and trying to persuade some people, through proper tactics, that it's the right vision.

We heard a wonderful vision before, which was to get away from military production and start thinking about alternative means. That's one image—and don't think only of that image. There are a lot of different images that planners have.

Cicchetti: I don't have problems with changing priorities, but I do have difficulty with someone deciding what the optimal priority will be.

Davidoff: It's all right to think about it and suggest to people. It's all right if the political platform says I think this is the best thing. That's different than imposing something.

Roberts: I think we're saying directions are great; end states are a little more dangerous.

Davidoff: There's no danger in thinking about end states. I think we get so fearful of central power imposition that we are fearful of even thinking about it. The question is the proper method for achieving that state. One end state that we've been talking about is redistribution—or maybe that's the process state. One of the problems with redistribution and programs to halt growth is that, politically, it's going to be very difficult to achieve redistribution in a situation where there's a static condition.

If we're going to be serious, as some of us are, about achieving an equality of opportunity in society, or an equity, then I think we have to recognize that to do it in a stage of non-growth is going to be impossible in our political situation, except perhaps by some revolutionary means. If we wish non-revolutionary means to achieve greater equity, then I think we must recognize that no-growth makes that increasingly more difficult.

Cicchetti: Talk about visions frightens me because I would rather have us change the things that we see are wrong—that is, change the excess use of electricity and the pricing arrangement that encourages it, or change things that say we use resources at a very rapid rate because we have certain pricing policies.

I'd rather hear people say, let's plug up those things, like loopholes, the things that are making the system wrong for everyone but a small special-interest group. When people say that, I'm in perfect agreement. I'd certainly like to do that.

But not when it goes on to the other extreme and says, now that we've done all those things to correct the wrongs, we can now make a positive blueprint of society or the future. Whether people should be making violins or walking around in the forest—that kind of view I just don't know how to deal with.

Borrelli: Without a vision of some sort, we can misdirect a lot of our energies. There are lots of ways of attacking problems. We can conceive of as many taxes as there are dollars. We can, if we buried our heads within the federal bureaucracy, find a massive network of past policies and objectives that we could spend the next fifty years reversing. What we somehow have to do is arrive at a quality campaign, or some basic things that we go after, and let the other things trickle away and be changed by the technocrats and the bureaucrats.

Rooney: What I feel Charles [Cicchetti] is saying is that what we should be interested in is the planning process. If the planning process is democratically carried out in all that that might mean, then we can be open-ended about where we're going and our visions and our goals, because that is really what we're all struggling with. We all have this vision, we all have great deep concern for where we're headed or we wouldn't be here.

CHAPTER VIII

Redefining Economic Growth

Hazel Henderson
Consultant on Environmental Affairs
Princeton, New Jersey

AS ENVIRONMENTAL PROBLEMS become more manifest and pressures
to address them more insistent, it will be increasingly urgent for economists
to tackle the Gordian Knot of new questions surrounding the issue of
economic growth. The new questions concern, on the one hand, the
price in social and environmental exploitation which we pay for economic
growth, as defined by such indicators as the Gross National Product, and,
on the other hand, the companion question of how we should distribute
the costs and benefits of a new set of social arrangements geared toward a
"steady-state economy" in equilibrium with the ecosystem. These questions
are now challenging the basic concepts underlying traditional economic
thought.

In the United States, this debate began to surface in 1970, when
the environmental movement became visible as a potential political force.
The late George Wiley, at that time director of the National Welfare
Rights Organization, predicted the shape of the new debate in a speech
given at Harvard University on that first Earth Day:

> Are you going to ask the poor people of this country to bear the
> cost of cleaning up air pollution and doing something about other
> environmental problems? In all likelihood, a good many of the
> approaches that you are likely to take are going to be paid for directly
> at the expense of the poorest people in this country. This will happen
> in a number of ways. It will happen, for example, because most of the
> systems for controlling air and water pollution, if they are imposed,
> will simply be passed on to the consumer in higher costs. The poor
> people . . . will essentially be given a regressive tax. Is the ecology

movement planning to place any serious priority on the problems of the environment of the ghetto and the barrio, of our urban areas where pollution is worse? You must not embark on programs to curb economic growth without placing a priority on maintaining income, so that the poorest people won't simply be further depressed in their condition, but will have a share and be able to live decently.[1]

This new debate demands more attention to the distribution of wealth, which is too often accepted as a given in economic studies, as well as reevaluating natural resource factors of production, many of which—such as air and water—have hitherto been considered "free goods." Lest we assume that this problem of producers not paying for such resources as air and water is a feature only of capitalistic, market-oriented economies, we might note that in the Soviet Union land is often treated as a "free good." In fact, in both market-oriented and centrally directed economies, economic planners will have to redefine such ubiquitous economic concepts as "profit," "economic growth," "efficiency," "maximizing," "costs," "benefits," "productivity," and many other such value-laden terms. As we begin to see the normative nature of economics, we may be able to break out of the hypnotic circle of one-dimensional economic imagery which has almost dominated national decision-making since the Keynesian revolution some 35 years ago.

The Keynesian Legacy

A little historical perspective may be useful at this point. In the past, economists did not exert the great influence over the rhetoric of public policy-making that they do today. In 1936, John Maynard Keynes published *The General Theory of Employment, Interest and Money*, and his heady concepts of macro-economic management gave economists their first opportunity to grasp the reins of public policy.[2] No longer did they need to bow to the invisible hand of Adam Smith's atomistic world. Economists were able to take Keynes's Olympian view of whole national economies and how employment levels were related to levels of savings, investment and spending, and begin to persuade political leaders of the possibilities of manipulating these levels to sustain desired levels of general economic activity and employment. This Keynesian revolution produced great humanitarian benefits. No longer did economists stand by and wring their hands when a depression occurred with all its attendant human misery. Keynes showed that an economy could sink into a state of equilibrium at very low levels of employment and production, and just not budge unless policy-makers intervened to "prime the pump" with government spending and other measures.

From Keynes's liberating, macro-economic concepts of sustaining an economy at a chosen level, it was but a short leap to the idea of creating a pattern of continual growth. Such a set of policies, designed to institu-

124

tionalize economic growth, would "solve" a lot of social problems, particularly one of interest to a professed egalitarian democracy such as the United States: namely, greater equality in distribution of wealth and income. The beauty of institutionalizing economic growth was that it promised to overcome the biggest stumbling block in human history to fairer distribution of resources: those age-old conflicts inherent in the proposition that "if you get more, then I will get less." If the total economic pie could be made to grow continually, the thinking went, then the rich could keep their cake and be relieved of guilt—through the knowledge that the poor would eventually get theirs. Not only that, there was even a rationalization for some inequity in distribution because some people would have to be rich enough to have capital left over to invest so that new employment opportunities could be created.

This "trickle-down" theory, in broad terms, is the underlying premise on which our U.S. economy currently operates. Economists of the classical school were, at first, resistant to the policies of macro-economic intervention, but today even conservative Milton Friedman cheerfully admits that "we are all Keynesians now."

In all disciplines, and in society as a whole, there is a lag time between the perception of a new set of conditions and the needed reconceptualizing of the old paradigms which fitted the previous set of conditions. As the Keynesian imagery caught hold, the economic policies it suggested became more euphoric. Not only did we not have to worry about the distribution of the fruits of our economy, but new technology, automation, and rising productivity would eventually overcome even physical-resource restraints. By the 1960s, some socio-economists saw little standing in the way of universal abundance and general hedonism. Production must be increased as fast as possible, investment levels must not be allowed to fall. Increasing aggregate consumption—fueled, if necessary, by the creation of wants through advertising—was the flywheel that kept the economic engine turning. And rises in the GNP became the overall symbol that all was moving onward and upward.

The trouble was that, as with all aggregate measures, the GNP could not differentiate between different kinds of production or investments, nor what goods and services they produced, nor what sort of jobs were created in the process. SSTs and ABMs, liquor, hair oil, and plastic novelties were lumped together with houses, education, and mass transit; channelizing a stream or writing cigarette commercials were considered comparable with producing food, clothing, or operating essential public services. Likewise, mechanizing and automating production lines became imperative to increase productivity while, at the same time, job satisfaction declined, many low-skill jobs disappeared, and natural-resource depletion rates rose.

Of course, any intelligent citizen could see that the underlying economic signalling system was no longer sufficiently refined and differentiated to program economic activity with the level of rationality needed to manage the vast complexities of a modern industrial economy. The notion that the planet's resources might not always be equal to the task of sustaining such helter-skelter economic activities came as a rude shock to many economists. Amid the euphoria, John Kenneth Galbraith's *The Affluent Society*, [3] first published in 1958, questioned the apparent over-supply of frivolous consumer goods in the private sector, while observing that, in the public sector, air and water were becoming polluted, parks and open space were diminishing, and cities were decaying.

In the previous chapter of this book, Sam Love points out one historical root of this lack of concern for resource factors. While Karl Marx spent a lifetime documenting the social exploitation that occurred when private profits were permitted without reckoning their larger social costs in human misery, he paid scant attention to the concomitant exploitation of resources. Indeed, he imputed all value in finished products to the role of human labor. This myopia concerning resource factors was natural, from Marx's time perspective; indeed, his labor theory of value grew out of concepts put forth in the beginning of the 19th century by the classical economist David Ricardo. The ratio of population to resources at that time, as well as the labor-intensive methods of resource exploitation, made nature's raw materials seem plentiful. Vast lands were unexplored, and it seemed that only human will and effort were needed to fashion the dross of earth, rocks, and water into the gold of finished goods. As time passed, economists gradually discredited this labor theory of value in favor of a more balanced view of the values of land, capital, and labor as inputs to production.

The Price of Everything

During World War II, when it was necessary to mobilize the entire economy, the new economic priesthood, now entrenched in Washington, gravitated close to the center of political power. Because of their arcane language, which precluded ordinary citizens from understanding much of the debate, they had managed to force the imagery and rhetoric of public policy into the straitjacket of cost-benefit analysis and other economic preconceptions. As Oscar Wilde said at the turn of the century, it was possible to know the price of everything and the value of nothing.

But the manifestations of their one-dimensional discipline became increasingly visible. The dichotomies grew: if budget messages were considered economically correct, they were socially and politically unacceptable; if they were socially and politically realistic, the economists railed against them with equal vigor. By the mid-1960s, the social anomalies of poverty, hunger, racial discrimination, and increasing crime and conflict in the materially richest country on earth had already become widely evident. And by 1970, the pollution of the air, water, and land had finally reached the sensory awareness of millions of Americans.

Today, we stand largely aware of the fact that the GNP is not (and in fairness to its inventor, Simon Kuznets, was never intended to be) an overall measure of human welfare. Economists have begun to address the problem of how to improve the GNP and to devise new social indicators of human welfare. James Tobin and William Nordhaus have devised an experimental Measure of Economic Welfare (MEW)[4] to replace the GNP. The MEW corrects for urban disamenities; reclassifies education and health expenditures as capital investments, thereby recognizing their value to society; and imputes value to leisure and non-market work, such as housework and voluntary services. Shigeto Tsuru, of Hitotsubashi University in Tokyo, suggests that we reformulate GNP along the lines first suggested by I. Fisher, in *The Nature of Capital and Income,* in 1906.[5]

Fisher, as Kenneth Boulding has also pointed out, made the economic distinction between stocks and flows in systems, which is also familiar to sys-

---

"The dichotomies grew: if budget messages were considered economically correct, they were socially and politically unacceptable; if they were socially and politically realistic, the economists railed against them with equal vigor."

---

tems analysts and physical scientists. Capital represents stock, and income the flow of wealth. Fisher declared that social wealth consists not only of producers' capital, such as plant and equipment, but also common property resources. In his scheme, "production" is defined as an addition to this social wealth, and "consumption" as a subtraction from it.

Thomas Juster, in the 50th Annual Report of the National Bureau of Economic Research, also reformulates GNP to include the following as capital: knowledge, physical environment, and what he calls "socio-political assets."[6] And most interesting of all, perhaps, the Japanese are in the process of changing to a new set of national socio-economic indicators, called not GNP, but NNW—the *Net National Welfare.*

These new efforts underline Charles Cicchetti's observation that an economic signalling system which rewards activities with individual or corporate profit in spite of the unaccounted social and environmental losses they incur must be overhauled with vastly greater information about these losses—losses which economists term, in what might almost be a Freudian slip, "externalities." These externalities, now familiar to most environmentalists, consist of everything the entrepreneur would like to exclude from his balance sheet. They can be social in nature (e.g., inadequate plant safety) or environmental (e.g., pollution and resource depletion).

In fairness, it must be noted that as far back as the Victorian England of the 1890s, Alfred Marshall, the great economist and teacher of John Maynard Keynes, introduced the concept of externalities. Marshall was attempting to break out of the type of economic thinking that treated the economy as a closed equilibrium system—by showing that external forces affected economic activities. The outside forces he drew attention to were mostly of a positive nature, such as the rising level of health or education of the work force to which the entrepreneur of the day had contributed nothing —often due to public investments of taxpayer's money. A. C. Pigou, the man who succeeded to Marshall's chair of political economy at Cambridge, became interested in the idea that there could also be *negative* externalities, as he watched smoke pour out of an English factory chimney.

But the concept of externalities remained rather a theoretical abstraction—an empty box on the diagrams of economic model-makers—until K. W. Kapp published his *Social Costs of Private Enterprise* in 1950.[7]

"The task now is to begin filling that empty box marked 'externalities' with some solid data documenting these social and environmental diseconomies. For, inasmuch as they can be quantified or reasonably approximated, and companies can be forced through law or public pressure to internalize them as true costs of production, prices of those products with the heaviest social costs will rise."

It was Kapp's central thesis that the maximization of net income by microeconomic units (entrepreneurs, corporations, etc.) was likely to reduce the income or utility of other economic units and of society at large, and that conventional measurements of the performance of an economy were misleading. Interestingly, Jay Forrester, in his book *World Dynamics* (1971),[8] translates this statement into an axiom concerning the behavior of large non-linear systems: the optimization of any given subsystem will generally be in conflict with the goal of optimizing the macrosystem of which it is a part. We might paraphrase this idea as "what's good for General Motors is not very likely to be good for America"—something that the anti-highway groups have been trying to tell us.

The task now is to begin filling that empty box marked "externalities" with some solid data documenting these social and environmental diseconomies. For, inasmuch as they can be qualified or reasonably approximated, and companies can be forced through law or public pressure to internalize them as true costs of production, prices of those products with the heaviest social cost will rise. Working effectively, such an approach will serve as a rationing device. The price of block-long automobiles or snowmobiles or beach buggies would rise astronomically, once all their social costs were calculated into the price.

But what about the impact of internalized costs on the price of essential commodities, and the effect of this on the poor? Here we face the nub of our dilemma. All economic systems are rooted in social systems, and the current structure of our social system is the key in determining how these costs will be shaved. Therefore, economic data which ignore social structure can lead to inequitable burdens on the poor.

While resource economists—such as Allen V. Kneese, Robert Havermann, Charles Cicchetti, Ronald Ridker, and others—have been documenting these environmental externalities and providing valuable information to improve economic models and permit the price system to carry more of the load of rationing scarce resources, another group—generally referred to as welfare economists because of their interest in the human aspects—has begun to examine how these higher prices will affect the distribution of income and how pollution controls may affect employment in marginal plants and the economy in general.

Both types of economic studies are necessary if we are to have more accurate answers to both resource and welfare questions. However, while the welfare questions can easily be apprehended by the great body of traditional economists—so much so that these distributional questions are being used as an argument for the status quo and doing nothing about environmental problems—the new resource-scarcity questions are mind-boggling to most economists. Even Tobin and Nordhaus, who have tried to make GNP more sensitive to such disamenities as urban pollution and congestion, flatly state that there is little reason to worry about the exhaustion of resources.

The Specter of Scarcity

Even though incipient resource scarcities and overexploitation have been documented, this documentation has frequently been done by scientists, not by economists. It has tended to remain outside the economists' agenda or has been dismissed as a phenomenon that prices could handle adequately when the time came. This situation began to change with the environmental movement's growth in political power and with the publication of two books that attempted yet another series of heroic aggregations:

Jay Forrester's *World Dynamics* in 1971, and *The Limits to Growth*, by Dennis Meadows and others, in 1972.[9] These books attempted to computer-model, on a global scale, the interactions of such variables as population, food supply, geographical space, capital investment, pollution and resource depletion, and their behavior over time.

Although economists generally scoffed at the studies, or sharply criticized their extremely large aggregations and other methodological factors, they had to address the population/resource/distribution issues Forrester and Meadows raised, simply because they created such an impact that they entered the realm of political debate and action. Gradually, some economists —such as Henry Wallich and others with intellectual investments in the economic growth paradigm—began to address the issues more calmly. Their first evaluations dismissed the studies as new Malthusian scares, and went on to say that since Malthus's dire predictions of food shortage and over-population—made 150 years ago—had not yet occurred (famines are still localized), they were unlikely to occur in the future: a somewhat shaky linear extrapolation. It was also claimed that technological innovation and the substitution of new materials would continue, as specific resources became scarcer, because prices would rise. In essence, this is the "Apollo syndrome" to which Cicchetti refers—a faith that technology, like God, will provide.

The Fallacy of the Ever-Expanding Pie

The real nub of the growth issue—the question of distribution—is revealed by the economists' contention that economic growth (persumably as currently defined) must continue, since it is the only way to provide increasing shares of the pie to the poor. Economists often cite studies by Robert Lampman on the correlation between economic growth and increase in welfare, showing a 37 per cent gain in real per-capita consumption between 1947 and 1962. But two recent studies challenge these assertions on the grounds that relative patterns of distribution among groups in the economy have remained unchanged. Lester Thurow and Robert Lucas, of the Massachusetts Institute of Technology, claim that in 25 years of steady economic growth, the income shares are essentially the same in 1970 as they were in 1947.[10]

Even more disturbing is a study by Peter Henle, of the U.S. Department of Labor, which notes a persistent trend in our economy toward actual inequality: for example, from 1958 to 1970, the share of aggregate wage and salary income earned by the lowest fifth of male workers declined from 5.10 per cent to 4.60 per cent, while the share of the highest fifth of male wage and salary earners rose from 38.15 per cent to 40.55 per cent. Henle did not see this trend as a nefarious plot against the poor; he concluded only that the structure of our economy was producing more high-paying, high-skill jobs, while low-skill employment remained constant.[11]

130

This central issue of distribution of wealth, whether under our current institutional patterns or a new set of relationships geared toward a new steady-state economy in equilibrium with the biosphere, was a crucial concern of the Woodstock Conference participants. Cicchetti cites studies, prepared for EPA, which forecast price rises of as much as 10 per cent as a result of more stringent environmental controls. As Peter Borrelli and John Yolton pointed out, however, this is small comfort to the worker in a marginal plant that gets phased out on a faster schedule.

Though we know that new industries often take up some of the slack in the labor market—an example is the growth of the pollution-control industry, which has added some 850,000 new jobs to the economy—labor economists have long recognized that the labor market does not always function well in matching new job opportunities with job seekers. They have recognized barriers to the mobility of workers, often trapped in depressed areas; discrimination for reasons of race or sex; and lack of information as to where and what the new job opportunities are. These and other factors—such as technological change, new production and distribution methods, government policies affecting interest rates, railroad abandon-

---

"The point is that environmental policies, whether geared to stricter controls or not, will do little to alter the major contours of employment in this country one way or the other if all of the other structural and policy factors remain unchanged."

---

ments, changing consumer tastes, public works projects, and the private decisions of corporations on location of new facilities—influence the job market much more than do environmental-protection measures.

Therefore, it is unrealistic to single out cases of plant closings, even when they are accurately attributed to environmental-control costs. Preventing them from occurring in the short run will not prevent their subsequent phasing out for more familiar reasons of obsolescence; nor would it forestall the vaster array of larger factors from continuing to operate with much greater effect on employment.

Other factors affecting workers include all manner of government measures to control the rate of inflation, which most economists believe is intrinsically related to high levels of employment.

The point is that environmental policies, whether geared to stricter controls or not, will do little to alter the major contours of employment in

131

this country one way or the other if all of the other structural and policy factors remain unchanged. Keith Roberts draws our attention to the problems generated by those institutional frameworks and power relationships that often perpetuate inequities, and to how new legislation and new agencies, formed with the best of intentions, can end up subsidizing the wrong people. We need only look at the familiar story of our regulatory agencies, which have tended to become captured by the industries they were established to regulate. Zoning is another example of how an institutionally enforced system provides environmental protection against the poor, but no environmental protection against the rich.

And yet, as Scott Paradise notes, in spite of all the entrenched economic and political forces which narrow our range of options, we still must find ways of changing or deflecting the kind of destructive, short-term economic growth we are now experiencing. Its inherent instabilities, irrationalities, and costs are now catching up with it, and it is this fact that serves to make environmental-protection measures, which are vital in the long run, appear to be the straw breaking the camel's back.

A Resurgence of Grass-Roots Capitalism

The issue now confronting environmental groups is how to pick their way through our existing economic system so as to find points of leverage and intervention where they may advance environmental goals that parallel, rather than conflict with, the goals of labor, the poor, and those who suffer discrimination. In some areas, we see that it is possible to change government policies so that funds flow into such areas as mass transit and health care, which will help to graft new, less destructive sectors onto our economy and which can also provide new jobs.

Environmentalists can also join forces with the many divergent groups now calling for new national priorities. Such groups, and their recent growth, are a hopeful sign of growing public understanding of the interwoven economic causes underlying their concerns. People are now asking why jobs and institutions cannot be structured to perform tasks which address current conditions, rather than continuing in the outmoded patterns designed to meet an earlier set of needs and priorities.

Meadows and Forrester identify this kind of cultural and information lag in large social systems as the cause of the familiar "overshoot mode," where the system cannot be deflected from its original program until too long after events have outrun it. One might look at the gradual build-up in U.S. military budgets or the automobilization of the nation in this light. They are both complex, non-linear, and counter-intuitive systems, incorporating positive feedback mechanisms which permit them to grow exponentially.

132

In the case of the historical growth of the military, we see the enormous build-up needed during World War II, which created a new set of economic constituents: client corporations, subcontractors, military bureaucrats, and millions of jobs which, in turn, created political pressures to continue the upward spiral through Korea and Vietnam. Only very recently did the public distaste for the Vietnam war grow strong enough to begin generating negative pressures, and new steam behind the movement for new priorities and economic conversion to peacetime production.

Similarly, the growth of the automobile syndrome can be seen as a vast non-linear system which grew exponentially as the economic and political power of the auto companies and their economic dependents—the oil, rubber, steel, and highway-construction industries—grew large enough to control political processes and public-resource allocations (such as the Highway Trust Fund) to further consolidate their industrial complex. Just as recently, the automobile system has gone into an overshoot mode where it is now generating negative pressures. It can no longer deliver on its

---

"People are now asking why jobs and institutions cannot be structured to perform tasks which address current conditions, rather than continuing in the outmoded patterns designed to meet an earlier set of needs and priorities."

---

chief promise—individual mobility; and its delayed effects on air quality, human health, agriculture, and urban values are now becoming widely visible.

The new nexus issues, developing under the banner of new priorities and economic conversion to unmet human needs, are where environmentalists can work most equitably and effectively. Sam Love noted that Environmental Action has tried to focus on those environmental issues with distributional aspects, such as the utility industry with its heavy environmental effects and the regressive nature of its rate structure.

Other environmental coalitions might work to close tax loopholes, such as oil depletion allowances, the huge tax giveaways available in land speculation and development, or the corporate boondoggle provided by pollution-control bonds. Environmentalists and less-affluent Americans might join in development of "grass-roots capitalism" in community-based human service areas, such as entrepreneurial day-care operations run by local women who share "pieces of the action"; community cable TV franchises; or small health clinics using para-professionals.

The reason that promoting "grass-roots capitalism" would be an appropriate goal in environmental, as well as human, terms is based on the ecological principle that diverse, pluralistic systems seem to work better in nature, and—as Kenneth Watt, the systems ecologist, has noted—when diversity in ecosystems is reduced, not only do they become less stable, but the energy flows through them increase proportionately. The gargantuan growth of our economic enterprises reduces diversity and narrows consumer and societal options. While up to a certain size they can provide economies of scale, they also increase requirements for transportation, coordination, inventory, materials handling, and distribution.

Looking further ahead on distribution issues, we might pay more attention to Louis O. Kelso's universal capitalism concepts,[12] which seek to structure businesses so that every worker can own a piece of the action—an all-important portion of the stock of wealth (capital) from which income flows. Kelso's ideas are a capitalist's version of the revisionism now popular in Yugoslavia, where each factory is run by a workers' council at every decision-making level, including how to re-invest earnings of the enterprise. Kelso argues that, if capital is diffused throughout the working population by means of his Employee Stock Ownership Trusts, the workers (now also stockholders) will bring much broader perspectives with them and force corporations into a more egalitarian style of management, helping to break the grip of very large capital owners on economic decision-making.

Kelso also believes that concentrated capital has greater potential adverse environmental impact than does diffused capital. This question needs further study, but one need hardly illustrate the environmental impacts of large capital investments when we see huge urban complexes and oil-refining facilities rising up on all sides. When our society needs to capitalize larger-scale and more ecologically compatible projects for tomorrow's needs, Kelso argues, we should build the ownership of these enterprises into citizens without capital holdings, loaning such people their "stake" in perhaps a hypothetical "Peoples' Solar Energy Development Corporation," insured by a federal development loan.

All such schemes to widen the distribution of wealth—even those proved viable, such as Kelso's Employee Stock Ownership Trusts—will be considered by economists to be unfeasible or radical because they shatter old dogmas, particularly the one that economic development (whether environmentally destructive or benign) can only be the product of some existing capital owner's thrift, savings, and risk-taking, at least in the U.S. market-oriented economy. Kelso's most useful insight is that new economic activities can be freed from the slavery of past savings—that is, they can be financed like home mortgages, so that the new wealth and dividends they produce may be owned by anyone, rather than being pyramided exclusively by existing owners.

134

Toward An Equitable "Steady-State" Economy

An indication of the growing importance of the economic-distribution issue is the number of economists who are now addressing themselves to the equity implications of a new steady-state economy. Herman Daly believes that a steady-state society—with constant stocks of people and material wealth, maintained at some chosen rate of throughput—would require new institutions to maintain a floor under which incomes would not sink, as well as ceilings beyond which incomes could not rise and beyond which capital could not accumulate in individual hands.

The idea is hardly novel. As Sam Love points out, John Stuart Mill, in his *Principles of Political Economy*,[13] envisioned what he called a "stationary state" economy where distribution would become all-important. Here is what he wrote in 1848:

> I must confess that I am not charmed . . . by the trampling, crushing, elbowing and treading on each other's heels as the most desirable lot of humankind, or anything but disagreeable symptoms of one of the phases of industrial progress. It is only in the backward countries of the world that increased production is still an important object: in the most advanced, what is needed is better distribution, of which one indispensable means is stricter restraint on population.

Mill was also keenly aware of the political nature of all economic distribution. His great insight was that, once goods or any form of wealth have been produced, society—by its prevailing laws, customs, myths, and taboos—can place these goods at the disposal of whomever it pleases. Since the question of distribution is so central to environmental concerns, it is worth quoting Mill further on this subject:

> Even what a person has produced by his own individual toil, unaided by anyone, he cannot keep, unless by permission of society. Not only can society take it from him, but individuals could and would take it from him if society . . . did not . . . employ and pay people for the purpose of preventing him from being disturbed in his possession. The distribution of wealth, therefore, depends on the laws and customs of society. The rules by which it is determined are what the opinions and feelings of the ruling portion of the community make them, and are very different in different ages and countries, and might be still more different if mankind so chose. . . .

We have only to consider Indian potlatches and other such ritual distributions of goods to appreciate Mill's insight. Even the father of modern growthmanship, John Maynard Keynes, predicted in 1913 that "a point may be reached when (human) needs are satisfied in the sense that we prefer to devote our energies to non-economic purposes." In the same qualitative vein, E. J. Mishan, in *The Costs of Economic Growth*,[14] has drawn our attention not only to the destruction of amenities, but to the psychic losses we incur in the mad scramble for more goods.

Nevertheless, we must face the glaring question: In the immediate future, will the cost of environmental control fall most heavily on our poorer citizens? If we are honest, I believe we must admit that—without changes in our current institutional and power relationships—those with the least power and money will find themselves with a disproportionate share of the burden, just as they bear disproportionate burdens in our existing economic arrangements. It is the poor and unorganized who pay the greatest price for stemming inflation by more often losing their jobs. And it is the poor who bear the heaviest burden, in the form of health costs, of allowing the environmental problems to go unattended. Meanwhile, we have—as Bayard Rustin has said—"socialism for the rich and rugged individualism for the poor": a system that permits Lockheed Aircraft and the oil companies to receive generous government handouts, while the poor are hassled over food stamps, school lunch programs are dropped, and the War on Poverty is disassembled.

The poor have, up to now, been forced to trade their amenities, health, safety, and even their lives for their small piece of the economic pie. Unless we squarely face these arbitrary, socially determined distribution patterns and endeavor to change those that are unjust, the poor will likely pay just as heavily for the piecemeal, uncoordinated, and often conflicting environmental policies now being implemented.

New Measures of Efficiency

As long as capital is centralized in the hands of a very small proportion of our population, the rest of us must rely on the flows of wealth, i.e., income or welfare. This, as Herman Daly and Kenneth Boulding point out, is a major cause of the speed-up in the flows of production, consumption, waste or recycling (i.e., throughput), which must be kept circulating at high levels and continually increased to provide incomes and jobs for an increasing population.

Yet in an advanced economy, the production process is so interwoven with a complexity of factors—knowledge, management skills, government policies, taxes, incentives, and grants—that it is no longer possible for economists to say with confidence which rewards should accrue to labor and which to capital. Production of wealth is a social enterprise, based on such a tangled web of interrelationships that the old formula of "factors of production," leading to a logical distribution of its fruits among men, is now revealed as a fallacy.

An example of this fallacy can be found in energy-conversion performance. Is energy-conversion performance which permits the potential 60 per cent efficiency of a fuel cell (vis-à-vis the 12 per cent efficiency of an internal combustion engine) attributable to the physical equipment or to the man who operates it? Should the operator's wages be increased to reflect his increased "productivity"? Should we credit the man who invented the fuel cell, or the government grant which supported the university that supported his research? We might even include the efforts of his unremunerated wife who cooked his meals and maintained a tranquil home during his work. To whom does the fuel cell belong and who should share in its rewards?

The pathways through such a system of infinite interdependencies are unchartable with our current intellectual tools unless many assumptions are inserted into the economic models. For all practical purposes, we should admit that such innovations are social goods—and that their fruits should be distributed among people in light of this reality.

Let's take a moment to consider how these and other problems highlight the difficulties of designing accurate economic models. When the problem of infinite interdependencies is raised, the economist will answer

---

"The poor have, up to now, been forced to trade their amenities, health, safety, and even their lives for their small piece of the economic pie. Unless we squarely face these arbitrary, socially determined distribution patterns and endeavor to change those that are unjust, the poor will likely pay just as heavily for the piecemeal, uncoordinated, and often conflicting environmental policies now being implemented."

---

that his new tools of multiple-regression analysis are sharp enough to trace these relationships. But their economic terminology gives them away: the "regression" of these interdependent factors betrays their perspective—they are seen as receding, presumably in importance, until the economist decides on an arbitrary cut-off point. But the factors at the end of the chain of the economist's "regression" may, from some *other* perspective or disciplinary point of view, seem of central importance. It all depends where you see yourself in the system—that seamless web that preoccupies the perspectives of ecologists.

Another problem was pointed out by Paul Streeten, author of *Development in a Divided World*: "Cost/benefit analyses have a tendency to convert political, social and moral choices into pseudo-technical ones, hence its psychological appeal to administrators, but also its logical flaw, evident to

137

those trained in the analysis of choice." [15] If there is a set of conflicting objectives representing different value judgments and choices between a quantifiable objective, such as a new plastics factory, and non-quantifiable objectives, such as the local residents' preference for clean air, beaches, and water for fishing, then this choice can only be resolved politically. Of course, the various costs and benefits of the widest possible choice of alternatives can be presented for consideration, but only the participatory political process can resolve the value conflicts. The choice can be made by democratic, oligarchic, or dictatorial means, but we have found that central planning, heavily geared to the output of cost/benefit data, generally comes unstuck when it runs into feedback from unconsulted, but affected, areas of society.

On the other hand, the welfare economists, however well-meaning, are busy trying to look at the costs and benefits of pollution control and other environmental goals, using their marginal analysis in terms of the willingness

---

"Yet in an advanced economy, the production process is so interwoven with a complexity of factors—knowledge, management skills, government policies, taxes, incentives, and grants—that it is no longer possible for economists to say with confidence which rewards should accrue to labor and which to capital."

---

to pay for some standard of environmental quality, or the willingness to accept compensation for damage. As K. W. Kapp notes, this economic "compensation principle," as a criterion for environmental quality, leaves no doubt in anyone's mind that the common denominator is going to be money. Kapp continues: "The basically questionable point of departure consists in the fact that original physical needs for rest, clean air, non-polluted water and health, as well as the inviolability of the individual, are being reinterpreted in an untenable way as desires or preferences for money income." He also cites the income inequalities which undermine the validity of this compensation principle, as well as the individual's inability to ascertain the full range of short- and long-run costs and benefits of environmental improvement (or its further disruption) upon his health and well-being.

Another fault of the compensation principle, Kapp believes, is that "it does not lead to the systematic search (by research and development expenditures) for alternative non- or less-polluting technologies." The growing list of shortcomings in current economic concepts and methods was summed up in a witty broadside by economist Alan Coddington, who

138

believes, with Kapp, that the main body of economic thought is ill-suited to coming to terms with ecology. "It may even be the case," Coddington wrote, "that the greatest service economists can render to posterity is to remain silent." [16]

If money is an inadequate measure for harmonizing economic activities with the ecosystem, what new criteria might be devised to evaluate policy decisions which will face the citizens in some future steady-state economy? As a few daring economists begin to respond with new concepts which more accurately match new realities, we will see their discipline incorporate more hard data on resource factors and the unrewarded chemical exchange work provided by nature to maintain viable host ecosystems for human economic activities. Kenneth Boulding and Barbara Ward first drew our attention to these unrewarded natural cycles of ecosystems, powered by the sun, which must eventually provide all base-line data for economic models. Herman Daly has added useful insights, including the observation that young ecosystems, like young economies, are characterized by high production levels, while mature ecosystems, like mature economies, are characterized by high levels of maintenance activity.

In 1971, Howard Odum, author of *Environment, Power and Society,*[17] noted this inadequacy of economic terms to describe the chemical-exchange work and energy flows that occur in the real world. For example, Odum is now working on a "value system" calculated and converted from kilocalories to dollars, to enable a cost/benefit analysis to credit the chemical-exchange work performed by the host system of a proposed economic activity at the same rate that humans would have been paid for comparable work. This invisible, unaccounted activity includes, for example, absorbing carbon dioxide from combustion and replacing the oxygen that all such processes consume, or converting industrial wastes and sewage back into usable fuel or fertilizers. For, as we noted earlier, prices are arbitrary human exchange values derived from our subjective and still imperfect understanding of the actual exchange values of ecosystem processes and natural transactions.

Economist Nicholas Georgescu-Roegen's book, *The Entropy Law and the Economic Process,*[18] sets the problem of inadequate economic paradigms in a heroic space-time context in what may be the most important recent book on the ecology/economics debate. He notes, with sympathy, that economic activity is an evolutionary process which generally changes too fast for economists to keep up with. In his view, the trouble is that the overarching paradigm of economics pictures economic activities as analogous to Newtonian concepts of locomotion, which are linear, arithmetic, and reversible.

Not so, he goes on to say. On the contrary, economic processes are not reversible because they are part of the irreversible process of evolution, and they operate within the basic laws of physics: the first and second laws of thermodynamics. For example, once a piece of coal is burned and its bound energy has been used and dispersed through friction as waste heat, that particular piece of coal can never be reconstituted or burned again. Matter can be recycled, but only with inputs of energy, and energy utilization is always associated with entropy (i.e., energy itself can never be recycled).

One despairing physicist, after failing to get this concept across to a group of economists, related his favorite example of the unnecessary entropy our truncated money language permits: the almost sinful dispersion of the valuable resource, chromium, which is used to face the edges of razor blades that are then irretrievably pushed down those little slots in millions of U.S. bathrooms! Another example of national entropy is the sorry mess and waste created by the automobile and the conflicts over exhaust controls.

Georgescu-Roegen not only challenges the quantitative assumptions of the locomotion model of economic processes, but suggests that economics has fallen into what Alfred North Whitehead called "the fallacy of misplaced concreteness." Because the qualitative changes associated with greater entropy levels which all economic processes create are not easily modelled, economists tend to ignore them in favor of the easy processes which can be expressed arithmetically. This "arithmomania" causes economists to address increasingly irrelevant and simplistic problems—from which all those stubborn and intransigent variables are excluded so that the model will "work" in the approved Newtonian style.

Boulding cautions that "arithmetic should be an aid to, not a substitution for, thought." He also comments on the entropy problem, noting that economic activity is the process of segregating entropy: low-energy-level deposits of resources are processed with inputs of energy (human or nonhuman) into more improbable low-entropy goods, but only at a cost of even higher-entropy-level wastes somewhere else. Georgescu-Roegen states flatly that the low-level entropy represented in the finished goods is always less than the sum of the naturally occurring low-entropy resources used to fabricate them. He adds that, in entropy terms, all recycling is fruitless, since it consumes more energy, which is non-replaceable and non-recycleable. It may be amusing to note, at such a depressing juncture, that both economists and ecologists have always agreed on Barry Commoner's proposition: There Is No Such Thing As A Free Lunch. Now, the dismal second law of thermodynamics is forcing both groups into recognizing an even more dismal proposition: Each Lunch Costs More Than The Last.

One implication of the entropy law is that all economic processes must be modelled in their entirety—from extraction to fabrication to distribution to consumption to waste to recycling—with the objective of pinpointing any hidden energy subsidies along the way. Thermodynamicist Stephen Berry [19] has prepared such a model of the life cycle of the automobile, which leads him to conclude that the largest energy and "thermodynamic-potential" savings can be achieved in the basic method of metal recovery and

140

fabrication. This could, in principle, reduce the thermodynamic "costs" of automobiles by factors of five, ten, and more. By comparison, extending the life of a vehicle could realize thermodynamic savings of between 50 per cent and 100 per cent, whereas recycling can achieve a saving of some 10 per cent, and probably less by 1980.

Many other useful thermodynamic analyses are now being devised. Two recent examples were published in shortened articles in *Environment*. One, by Bruce Hannon,[20] found that throw-away bottles consume 3.11 times the energy of returnables. In the State of Illinois, he found that a complete

---

"It may be amusing to note, at such a depressing juncture, that both economists and ecologists have always agreed with Barry Commoner's proposition: There is no such thing as a free lunch. Now, the dismal second law of thermodynamics is forcing both groups into recognizing an even more dismal proposition: Each lunch costs more than the last."

---

conversion to returnables could also save consumers some $71 million annually—another case where the interests of consumers in lower prices meet with those of environmentalists, and where a corporate activity is creating an adverse distributional effect (since returnables are hard to find).

The other study, by A. B. Makhijani and A. J. Lichtenberg,[21] suggests that the usually accepted close correlation between standard of living (as measured by GNP) and per-capita energy consumption must be reassessed. It cited a 1964 U.S. government study that shows that eight industrial countries with similar standards of living (indicated by GNPs within 10 per cent of each other)—the United Kingdom, Australia, Germany, Denmark, Norway, France, Belgium and New Zealand—showed large disparities in energy consumption. The United Kingdom consumed 110 million BTUs per capita per year, while New Zealand consumed only 45 million BTUs per capita. Obviously, a large portion of the difference was accounted for by Britain's greater exports, but the disparity was striking enough to suggest questions of relative energy-conversion efficiencies. The study then calculated the total energy inputs for dozens of primary extraction and manufacturing processes and the energy content of the finished goods. From these data, they were able to identify those areas where energy-conversion efficiencies could be improved. They claim that, by employing the best mix of energy conservation methods, an advanced economy might be able to significantly reduce overall energy consumption without reducing its standard of living.

141

From such revaluation of resource inputs, economists may come to understand that economic and agricultural processes cannot continually substitute capital for human labor in order to raise "productivity." This drive to automate as labor costs rise has a heavy distributional effect: jobs are lost in the low-skill areas, causing greater impact on the poor than on the average worker. In addition, there are other important problems in increasing the capital-intensiveness of production processes, including the need in many less-developed countries to sacrifice "efficiency" for jobs and the reduction of conflicts over the maldistribution of wealth, which can be seen clearly as these countries try to emulate Western-style economic development. For example, Brazil, which is rapidly industrializing along Western lines, is experiencing increasing maldistribution of wealth, as well as unemployment, as formerly rural peasants flood into cancerously growing cities in search of jobs. Meanwhile, housing, transportation, and other social infrastructure costs rise amid deteriorating environmental conditions. And Japan's economic growth has caused so much environmental disruption that internal political unrest over this issue is forcing large expenditures to clean up some of the mess. Indeed, Barry Commoner's notion that fairer distribution of world resources is justified on humanitarian as well as ecological grounds was widely discussed at the UN Conference in Stockholm, as a new chance for poorer nations to better their economic positions by "capitalizing" their relatively less-devastated environments. However, they were alert to the dangers of this course, and aware of the extent to which increased natural production might obviate the need for pollution-producing manufacture of synthetic substances, such as artificial rubber, fibers, and plastics.

Some Third World nations are now beginning to question capital-intensive, Western-type industrial development, as typified in W. W. Rostow's *The Stages of Economic Growth*.[22] They see the Chinese model as more viable to emulate, not only because it utilizes their most abundant resource—people—but also because it might help them avoid the erosion of national autonomy, which is often the price of importing foreign capital. The new views of the Third World were well summed up in the Founex Report, prepared for the Stockholm conference.

> In the past, there has been a tendency to equate the development goal with the more narrowly conceived objective of economic growth as measured by the rise in Gross National Product. It is usually recognized today that high rates of economic growth do not guarantee the easing of urgent social problems. Indeed, in many countries, high growth rates have been accompanied by increasing unemployment, rising disparities in income—both between groups and between regions —and the deterioration of social and cultural conditions. A new emphasis is thus being placed on the attainment of social and cultural goals as part of the developmental process.[23]

142

Arthur Pearl of the University of Oregon, in a recent article in *Social Policy* entitled "An Ecological Rationale for a Humane Service Society," has come to the same conclusion:

> It is only in a human services society which is labor intensive, rather than capital intensive, that the resources of the Earth will be conserved and human resources be expended for the benefit of human beings. Such a society is less likely to breed war, racism and poverty; these are necessary concomitants of a capital-intensive society.[24]

He adds:

> In essence, we have a surplus of human beings and a shortage of non-renewable materials: thus, we have to reverse our historical view of efficiency. Those who cry that the ecological crisis is diverting us from a war on poverty, although correct about the ways in which environmental approaches are being commercially manipulated, fail to recognize that a genuinely ecological strategy is the only fundamental anti-poverty approach possible in the present and future world.

All of these new issues lead to the need for a re-examination of cultural notions of value. For example, we in the United States tend to overvalue (and over-reward) competitive activities which can only exist within an equivalent field of cooperation and social cohesion. At the same time, we undervalue all the cooperative activities which hold a society together, such as child nurture and the vast array of services lovingly performed in the voluntary sector (and for which women bear an unfair burden of the opportunity costs).

Similarly, we and other Western countries tend to overvalue material wealth and to discount psychic wealth. As Walter Weisskopf points out, in *Alienation and Economics*,[25] the real dimensions of scarcity are not economic, but existential—that is, time, life, and energy, which, for man, are the ultimately scarce resources. These factors and needs are similar to those identified by psychologist Abraham Maslow: love, self-actualization, peace of mind, companionship, and time for contemplation and leisure. These needs can never be satisfied by purely economic means, although economic activity satisfies the more urgent needs for survival, thus permitting these new needs to emerge. In short, we humans tend to assign values arbitrarily based on our cultural myths and traditions, and then pay our measurers to collect only those data that conform to our assumptions of "value." The hypnotic circle is complete.

Some optimistic futurists claim we can beat the dismal entropy law by eventually reordering our solar system and capturing its energy for our use. Krafft Ehricke, an aerospace scientist with North American-Rockwell Corporation, envisions that we can make the Earth the residential planet of the solar system, while some planets can be mined for resources and others used for the disposal of our wastes. Who knows? He may be right in the long run. But we had better not count on it, or we may not be around for the luxury of such cosmic debates in the future.

Luckily, knowledge is not bound by the laws of physics. It can grow exponentially. Could it be that behaviorist B. F. Skinner is right—but on a scale he never imagined? Could it be that this planet is humanity's vast, programmed learning environment of positive and negative reinforcers? Could it be that, if we behave peacefully and cooperatively, we will be rewarded with survival? Could it be that, if we do not, the planet will restore itself to equilibrium by eliminating us? Perhaps, within Barry Commoner's riddle that ecological sanity requires social justice, there is hidden an equation representing "morality" for Earthians: Morality = Earth's matter + energy ÷ optimum population. If so, some future economists with global computer systems will be having the last laugh.

NOTES TO CHAPTER EIGHT

1. *Earth Day: The Beginning: A Guide for Survival,* Edited by the staff of Environmental Action, Washington, D. C.: 1971.
2. Robert Heilbroner, *The Worldly Philosophers,* Simon and Schuster, New York, 1961, Chap. 9, "The Sick World of Maynard Keynes."
3. J. K. Galbraith, *The Affluent Society,* Houghton & Mifflin, Boston, 1958.
4. *Selected Readings on Economic Growth in Relation to Population Increase, Natural Resource Availability, Environmental Quality Control and Energy Needs,* Prepared for the Committee on the Interior and Insular Affairs, U.S. Senate, Part II, Serial #92-3 September, 1971, pp. 67-69.
5. Irving Fisher, *The Nature of Capital and Income,* Macmillan Company, London/New York, 1906.
6. *Op. cit., Selected Readings on Economic Growth, etc.,* p. 167.
7. K. William Kapp, *The Social Costs of Private Enterprise,* Oxford University Press, 1950. New edition now available: Schocken Books, Inc., New York, 1971.
8. Jay W. Forrester, *World Dynamics,* Wright-Allen Press, Cambridge, 1971.
9. Dennis Meadows *et al.,* The Limits To Growth, Universe Books, New York, 1972.
10. *Business Week,* April 1, 1972, p. 56.
11. *New York Times,* December 27, 1972, p. 1.
12. Louis O. Kelso, *Two-Factor Theory: The Economics of Reality,* Vintage Pocketbooks, New York, 1967.
13. John Stuart Mill, *Principles of Political Economy,* John W. Parker & Sons, London, 1857.
14. Ezra J. Mishan, *The Costs of Economic Growth,* Praeger, New York, 1967.
15. Paul Streeten, "Cost Benefit and Other Problems of Method," Essay in *Political Economy of Environment: Problems of Method,* Proceedings of Conference in Paris, July 5-8, 1971, Mouton, The Hague/Paris, 1972.
16. Alan Coddington, Essay, "The Economics of Ecology," *New Society,* April, 1970, p. 595.
17. Howard Odum, *Environment, Power and Society,* Wiley Interscience, New York, 1971.
18. Nicholas Georgescu-Roegen, *The Entropy Law and the Economic Process,* Harvard University Press, Cambridge, 1971.
19. *Bulletin of the Atomic Scientists,* May, 1972, p. 8.
20. Bruce M. Hannon, "Bottles, Cans, Energy," *Environment,* March, 1972.
21. A. B. Makhijani and A. J. Lichtenberg, "Energy and Wellbeing," *Environment,* June, 1972.

22. W. W. Rostow, *The Stages of Economic Growth,* Cambridge University Press, 1966.

23. "Founex Report on Development and Environment," *International Conciliation,* January, 1972, Carnegie Endowment for International Peace.

24. Arthur Pearl, "An Ecological Rationale for a Humane Service Society," *Social Policy,* September-October, 1971, p. 40.

25. Walter Weisskopf, *Alienation and Economics,* E. P. Dutton & Co., New York, 1971.